SECRET
DARLINGTON

Chris Lloyd

AMBERLEY

About the Author

Chris Lloyd is the chief feature writer of *The Northern Echo* and the *Darlington & Stockton Times*, where his articles about local history, places and people are among the most read in paper and online. A former North East Journalist of the Year, his interest in local history was sparked around thirty years ago when, as a graduate of the University of St Andrews in Scotland, he was parachuted into Darlington – as a southerner, a town he had never visited before – as a trainee reporter. He set out to understand why the town existed and who and what had shaped it, and if there really was a difference between a railway engine and a railway train. Although he has mastered the latter, this is his ninth book in the unending quest to understand Darlington. He is known for his illustrated talks, walks and broadcasts, including his weekly slot on BBC Tees. He is married to Petra and they have two children, Genevieve and Theodore, who, on an outing, always enjoy having the brakes slammed on whenever an odd old thing is spotted and needs to be investigated.

First published 2020

Amberley Publishing
The Hill, Stroud
Gloucestershire, GL5 4EP

www.amberley-books.com

Copyright © Chris Lloyd, 2020

The right of Chris Lloyd to be identified as the Author of this work has been asserted in accordance with the Copyrights, Designs and Patents Act 1988.

ISBN 978 1 4456 9473 3 (print)
ISBN 978 1 4456 9474 0 (ebook)

British Library Cataloguing in Publication Data.
A catalogue record for this book is available from the British Library.

Origination by Amberley Publishing.
Printed in Great Britain.

Contents

Introduction

Darlington is said to be the tun, or settlement, of an Anglo-Saxon called Deortha, who, more than 1,000 years ago, settled on the banks of the River Skerne, a name which means 'bright' or 'shining'. Its unrecorded history, though, obviously goes back much further than that. For instance, in 2013, archaeologists at Faverdale unearthed, for the first time in nearly 2,000 years, a surprisingly extravagant British farmstead, which even included a two-roomed building with hypocaust underfloor heating. Hidden for two millennia was a pottery drinking cup from southern Gaul on which the owner had scratched his name: Januarius.

Januarius, therefore, is the first known named Darlingtonian, even though he lived many centuries before Deortha showed up and settled down.

This book is an attempt to unearth some more secrets of Darlingtonians and their town. In many ways it is a companion to my previous book for Amberley, *Darlington in 50 Buildings*, which, as the title suggests, tells the stories of fifty of the town's most prominent buildings. This book, then, is a look at the people who have lived, worked, played and worshipped in and around those buildings.

It attempts to work out why they joined Deortha in settling on the banks of the shining river as the town developed into the mercantile and agricultural capital of south Durham and North Yorkshire. Then the town provided people with employment making textiles as it became a centre of continental renown before it invented the modern railway – a feat of ingenuity for which it is famed around the world, although, modestly, it likes to keep its light hidden.

The book also looks at the stories of some of the most striking townspeople – people involved in scandals, or who performed heroic deeds or led great campaigns, or who have a remarkable, if highly unlikely, claim to fame. Who would have thought that the first and only World Pouff-Dart Champion could come from Darlington?

In helping to shine a light on some of these secrets, I am extremely grateful to the staff in the Darlington Centre for Local Studies, especially Katherine Williamson and Mandy Fay, for all of their assistance, and I am eternally grateful to the global audience of billions who read *The Northern Echo*'s Memories supplement every Saturday and overlook the myriad mistakes to contribute fascinating information and unimaginable twists to the story lines.

1. Coat of Arms

Darlington's coat of arms is central to this multiview postcard, which was posted in March 1916.

Darlington's first coat of arms was sketched in 1868, when the town's first democratic council was created, but due to an oversight it was not completed for ninety-two years.

Darlington

Finally, in 1960, Darlington's coat of arms was professionally drawn, flanked by a regal lion and the Sockburn Worm skewered by a falchion.

An Edwardian postcard of High Row with the sketchy coat of arms in the bottom left-hand corner.

A study of Darlington's coat of arms is a good starting point in a quest to understand the town's secrets. The emblem was drawn up – well, amateurishly sketched, to be more accurate – in 1867 when, after an acrimonious battle in which the ruling Quaker families of the Peases and Backhouses were forced to accept the bright light of democracy, Queen Victoria granted the town a charter of incorporation.

The charter gave the town the right to run its own affairs through its first one-man-one-vote town council. At the first meeting, a competition was announced – with a first prize of five guineas – to create a coat of arms that symbolised the character and history of the proud new borough.

The winner was a joint submission by civil engineer Robert Robinson, of Beechwood, in Grange Road (where Sainsbury's supermarket is today), and G. Fryer of Smelt House, Howden-le-Wear. Their rough drawing showed a bull, which symbolised the town's role as the agricultural market town of south Durham and North Yorkshire; three bales of wool, to show how the town's prosperity was based on the textile industry; and a curious-looking trainset, which was supposed to suggest how the town had been the birthplace of the world's first modern railway. They even added a motto: '*floreat industria*' – 'let industry flourish'.

They must have hoped their rough sketch would be polished into an imposing emblem but the town council failed to register the design with the College of Arms, and so, although the coat of arms was widely used, it remained in rough sketch form. It wasn't until the 1950s that the townspeople's agitation led to a professionally drawn coat of arms being registered in London in 1960. The sketch was then enhanced to give it the grandeur befitting a borough as proud of its history as Darlington. The bull became the sort of a noble creature likely to be found in an agricultural capital; the bales were tidied up to represent a European textile capital, and the locomotive finally looked like the world-famous Stockton & Darlington Railway's epoch-making *Locomotion No. 1*. To complete the arms, a regal lion was added on one side and a frighteningly ferocious dragon on the other – although the poor thing does have a falchion, or sword, through its neck to represent the legend of the Sockburn Worm.

So, prior to this, for the best part of a century, the 'borough arms' of Darlington was a sketchy affair featuring a soppy and mangy bull, a square and static railway engine and three bales of wool that were so badly drawn that they have been misinterpreted by those who wish to poke fun at the Quaker temperance town as being three barrels of ale, apparently symbolising Darlington's regular enjoyment of a good drink.

However, for all its artistic faults, the borough arms – which was replaced in 1974 when the town became a district of County Durham – do shed light on those early secrets of the town...

DID YOU KNOW?
The Sockburn Worm – the Old Norse word 'orm' means 'dragon' – was probably a Viking invader who took up residence south of Darlington and was raping, pillaging, burning and blaspheming until brave Sir John Conyers, inspired by the Holy Spirit, sliced through him with a heavy sword, or falchion. That falchion is presented to every new Bishop of Durham as he crosses the Tees into his diocese as a symbol of the strength of the area's faith.

2. Market Town
and Agricultural Capital

St Cuthbert's Church, which Bishop Hugh de Puiset began in the early twelfth century, probably on top of an older Saxon church.

A time-honoured view across the broad, open Market Place towards St Cuthbert's Church.

An Edwardian postcard showing the Market Place crowded with stalls and people.

The soft and rather mangy-looking bull on the borough arms represents Darlington's role from the eleventh century as the agricultural and commercial capital of much of County Durham and North Yorkshire. Initially, the market was held fortnightly on a Monday for seven months of the year between Whitsun and Christmas.

From the earliest days, it attracted customers from afar; in 1392, for example, the prior of Lindisfarne visited to buy some cows. It must have felt humiliatingly busy for John de Alwent (Alwent is a deserted medieval village just south of Staindrop), who admitted to Bishop Richard Kellaw, of Durham, in 1311 that he had committed adultery with Agnes de Raby and Annabella de Durham. John also failed to prove that he had not committed similar naughtiness with Christiana Clergis, Annabella de Castle Barnard and Emma le Aumbelour, so the bishop sentenced him to be dressed in linen and whipped around Gainford parish church for six consecutive Sundays and then also around Darlington marketplace on six consecutive Mondays 'during that part of the day when it should be most thronged'.

The Bishop of Durham was in charge of the market, and he employed a representative – the bailiff – to ensure everything ran smoothly and to collect all the tolls, tariffs and rents that were due.

Over the centuries, an army of bureaucrats grew up to run the bishop's market – and collect his money. He took a cut from every transaction, and employed heavies at every town centre gate to search people entering and leaving. By the seventeenth century he employed two constables 'for the searching and weighing of bread', two searchers of black leather, two searchers of red leather, two searchers of weights, plus tasters of ale, bread and butter, and four affeerors, who went round collecting fines from those who had displeased the bishop, in Darlington.

DID YOU KNOW?
Dame Dorothy Brown, who paid for Darlington's Market Cross in 1727, had three husbands. She married Michael Blackett, of Morton Palms and Newcastle, in 1683. After his death, she married barrister Sir Richard Browne in 1688, but the next year he was slain in Flanders by a Colonel Billingsley (how we wish we knew why). Her third husband, of 1694, was Rt Revd John Moore, the Bishop of Ely. They had three sons – two of whom became bailiffs of Darlington – and when the bishop died in 1714, he had 29,000 books, the largest collection in the country, which is now in Cambridge University Library.

In 1621, the bishop ordered that his ale tasters on Darlington market must do their job more diligently or be fined 3s 4d; in 1756, he ordered his constables to prosecute all 'monopolists, profiteers, engrossers and regraters' on the market.

These bureaucrats and the bailiff were based in the tollbooth at the top of the market. From the twelfth century, municipal operations like the courthouse and police cell naturally collected in the bailiff's tollbooth and so it developed into the first town hall.

The tollbooth where the bishop's army of bureaucrats had offices for around 900 years until it was replaced by the Italianate town hall in 1808. The buildings behind it are Horsemarket.

The goose market in Prospect Place was the last live market to leave the town centre.

As well as being a place to buy provisions, the market was famed for its animal sales. High Row specialised in cattle sales, sheep were sold in Tubwell Row (in 1851, the Queen's Head pub in Tubwell Row gave its address as 'the Sheep Market'), pigs went outside St Cuthbert's churchyard, geese flocked to Prospect Place and horses were sold in both Horsemarket and Bondgate.

The Market Cross is now in Horsemarket.

The top of the Market Cross – do you think the stonemason left the final 'e' off Browne and stuck it up above?

You could buy any animal on Darlington mart. In 1826, when a feline epidemic wiped out most of the district's cat population, an entrepreneur set up a cat stall selling moggies shipped in from elsewhere. Their prices ranged from 8*d* to 18*d*, depending on their age and beauty.

Indeed, any animal: 'hirings' markets, when servants were hired for the forthcoming season, were held on the Mondays before and after Mayday, and on the Mondays before and after Martinmas (St Martin's Day on 11 November).

Those wishing to be hired would gather on the steps of the Market Cross and wait for a wealthy homeowner or a landowner to pick them.

A market cross was the symbol of a town's right to hold a market and also a reminder in stone to the buyers and sellers of 'the sanctity of the bargain'. A cross – really just an impressive column – had stood in the centre of the marketplace since at least 1313 when Bishop Kellaw ordered a proclamation be read from its steps informing the people that unlicensed jousting was banned.

The current cross, which stands in Horsemarket, was a gift to the town by Dame Dorothy Browne in 1727. She was a Sadberge lady whose ancestor, Richard Barnes, had been Bishop of Durham in the late sixteenth century, so the lucrative role of bailiff had been passed down her family tree for more than a century, and she passed it to her husbands and then to her sons.

Her cross, which replaced a badly weathered stone, is splendidly carved, its beautifully spaced lettering still perfectly legible after nearly 300 years. Around the top it says: 'This crosse Erected by Dame Dorothy Brown 1727'. It appears, though, that for all the mason's clever chisel work, he was not much good at spelling, because he has had to put in arrow pointing up to a little 'e' which he has had to squeeze in to correct his spelling of Dame Dorothy's surname.

Italianate town hall of 1808, with the Market Cross standing at the top of Tubwell Row on the left. Behind it is the Shambles, or meat market.

As the nineteenth century wore on, the appeal of having a market run by an old-fashioned Prince Bishop with animals 'gorming' around the town centre began to wear thin. The bishop was the first to go – in 1856, the Board of Health (Darlington's first vaguely democratic town council) agreed to buy him out for £7,885 (about £850,000 in today's values). For this, the Board – dominated by the Liberal Party and the Quaker Pease and Backhouse families – got the Italianate town hall, built in 1808, and the shambles – or meat market, built alongside it in 1815 – plus the right to levy all the tolls and taxes.

At first, the townspeople were in favour of taking control of their own affairs, but then the Board of Health proposed building a more hygienic covered market with a larger town hall and an impressive clock tower.

DID YOU KNOW?
The clock in Darlington market's iconic clock tower was made by Thomas Cooke of York. It was hand-wound three times a week, taking seventy turns on a huge handle to raise the two lead weights to the top of the tower until it was electrified in 1977.

The townspeople were aghast. Their forty-year-old town hall didn't need replacing; their rates didn't want wasting on making councillors comfy in a town hall, and they didn't like the idea of their broad and wide Market Place being built upon. A virulent campaign against it arose, which intensified when the Liberal Quakers on the board rejected local architects' plans and instead asked a thirty-three-year-old from Manchester, who just happened to be a Quaker, a Liberal and related via marriage to the Darlington Quaker families, to design the complex. Worse still, his first gargantuan plan was to cost £14,000 – more than three times as expensive as any local ideas.

His name was Alfred Waterhouse. He had done some fairly minor jobs on the Quakers' local mansions, and was largely unknown outside Manchester, yet he would have a profound and beneficial effect on the townscape of Darlington and become regarded nationally as the greatest Gothic architect of the Victorian era, noted especially for Manchester Town Hall (1868), the Natural History Museum in London (1873), and Eaton Hall (1870–82) in Cheshire for the Duke of Westminster, which was the most expensive house to be built in Britain in the nineteenth century.

But at the start of that long and illustrious career, he scaled down his original proposals to a more affordable cost of £7,815, but perhaps because of the controversy, local builders refused to tender, and so the contract was awarded to a Londoner called Randall Stap, who was building a covered market in Longton, Staffordshire.

Mr Stap began in July 1862 by advertising for thirty stonemasons, who went on strike in November because one of their number – a youngster – had done too much work. In 1863, the impatient Board of Health decided that the Northern Counties Fat Cattle and Poultry Society could hold its annual show in the market on 9 December – even though the clock tower had not risen above head height.

Not only was the board keen to get £50 rent from the society, but members hoped the prestige of the event would counteract the project's unpopularity, and also a member of the Pease family felt he had a good chance of winning the show's top prize.

'Everything was in what would be designated by anyone but a captious cynic as apple-pie order,' said the *Darlington & Stockton Times* (*D&ST*). 'In the gaslight, the New Market presented a very beautiful appearance.'

The entries for the show filled the market: '70 head of cattle, 39 pens of sheep, 23 of pigs, samples of grain and roots, eight hams and bacon, five of butter, one stand of implements, and 815 cages of poultry.'

However, the stars of the show were the fat cattle – mountains of beef bred for their enormity. The top prize, the Gold Challenge Vase, was awarded to James Stewart, of Aberdeen, whose huge ox was 90 stones heavier than the runner-up, which belonged to Joseph Whitwell Pease (eldest son of Joseph 'the High Row statue' Pease).

The judging complete, the public were allowed in. 'At two o'clock, the place was literally swarming, and the difficulty of moving about was felt by all, especially by the ladies, whose wide skirts increased the difficulty tenfold,' said the *D&ST*.

The newspaper reporter went over to inspect Mr Stewart's prize-winning monster. He wrote:

> We dipped our fingers into the soft, velvet sides of the prize ox and had just turned from it … when a sudden crash fell on our ears, and immediately before us, not more than three yards off, we perceived a wide chasm, and a number of men at the very brink transfixed for the moment with terror, and not knowing which way to turn.
>
> The cause was A FRIGHTFUL ACCIDENT AT THE SHOW.
>
> The flooring of the Market had given way, and fallen through to the ground level, carrying with it in its descent a number of men, happily no females, and three cattle – Nos 27, in the catalogue, Sir WC Trevelyan's, which won the second prize amongst crossbred oxen; 28, Mr Collingwood Lindsay Wood's, and 29, Mr James Thompson's.'

Fortunately, said the D&ST, which is known as the farmers' bible, none of the three cattle were harmed during their 12ft plummet into the market's cellars. Then, the paper turned its attention to the animals which were of secondary importance: the humans.

> There appeared to us eight or ten men writhing with pain and struggling to rise out of the midst of rubbish in which they so suddenly found themselves engulfed,' it said. The most seriously injured was 'Mr Robert Robson, farmer of Newton Morrell (near Barton), whose face was ashy pale, and whose leg appeared to dangle loosely as he was being carried out of the hole.

Dr William Haslewood said:

> We found a fracture of the right thigh bone with a lacerated wound through which the broken bone protruded.' So he tied the 55-year-old's legs together with towels and put him in a cab, which bounced him over the cobbles to a relative's house in Northgate.

There he was seen by another eminent medical man, Dr Stephen Piper.

> After attending to him, I told the family he could not live long and if he had any affairs to settle it should be done,' said Dr Piper. 'I administered stimulants, champagne, brandy, ammonia and all those things we usually give in such cases.

The *D&ST* reported that 'the dying man made a will of his property and then resigning himself to his fate, rapidly sank'. He died at 4.30 p.m. on Saturday 12 December. The inquest was held the following Thursday, and the jury concluded: 'We are of opinion that Robert Robson came to his death from injuries received by the ... breaking of a metal girder which in our opinion, founded upon the evidence given, was not of sufficient strength to bear the weight placed upon it.'

This pointed the finger of blame straight at the young architect. The town must have been on the verge of uproar – the scheme that no one had wanted, the design of which had been nepotistically awarded to someone no one had ever heard of, had now killed a popular farmer before it was even complete.

The board acted rapidly, and the following Wednesday Thomas Bouch, Alfred Kitching and 'a number of other scientific gentlemen' gathered in the New Market to pass judgement on the girders – Mr Kitching was the founder of the Whessoe engineering firm and the builder of the famous Derwent locomotive; Mr Bouch built brilliant railway viaducts in Teesdale and beyond.

Mr Waterhouse said how he'd designed each girder to support up to 35 tons and yet it snapped with only 12 tons of man and beef standing on it. During the scientific gentlemen's tests, 'one of the trial girders broke by a pressure of 26 tons on the centre, the other bent a little at that pressure, this showing that the section made by the architect was correct and that the unfortunate accident was caused by a flaw in the casting,' reported the *Darlington Telegraph*.

DID YOU KNOW?
In 1808, Darlington's leading townsmen borrowed £2,000 from two old ladies to build a new town hall, to the Italianate plans drawn by Samuel Wilkinson, of the King's Head hotel. The foundation stone was laid on 13 April 1808 by George Allan, of Blackwell Grange, and the townspeople celebrated with a day's public holiday.

This flaw, the men of science concluded, had been caused when a piece of ash had been rolled into the metal by local ironfounder Mr W Hodgson Davison – who was neither a Quaker, nor a Liberal, nor married to anyone with useful relatives.

He took the blame, and Mr Waterhouse was exonerated, but just to be on the safe side, extra pillars were added to prop up the market floor should the girders not really be strong enough.

John Wrightson, the landlord of the Sun Inn and a regular opponent of the temperance Quakers, made the first purchase at the Covered Market at 7 a.m. on 2 May 1864.

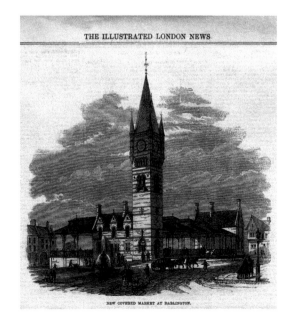

How the *Illustrated London News* illustrated the new market complex in Darlington in late 1864.

The market wasn't ready for opening until five months after the fatal accident. Local legend has it that the first purchase was made at 7 a.m. on 2 May by John Wrightson, the landlord of the Sun Inn, who bought a leg of mutton from Jack Crawford; it could be that Mr Wrightson, a vocal opponent of the ruling Quakers, had heard that the market was being quietly opened and so rushed down to make a fuss over the first purchase.

'There was no opening ceremony,' said that week's *D&ST*. 'The only official act was the apprehension of a couple of pickpockets who, by way of inauguration, tried their hands at a lady's pocket and got them into a pair of handcuffs.'

Within two months, the market was in full swing because on 16 July, stallholder William Walters was charged with breaking Market Bye-Law No. 55, which said: 'No person shall cry or shout his or her articles, goods, wares or merchandise.'

Despite being warned, Mr Walters 'persisted in crying out the merits of the articles he had for sale, bawling out to the great annoyance of other people'. He was arrested after 'calling out 'fourpence a pound for cherries' in such a loud voice that it could be heard right across the market'. Magistrates fined him 5s with 4s costs, or gave him the option of fourteen days imprisonment.

The market's distinctive clock tower was personally paid for by Joseph Pease, the head of the family and chairman of the board. It cost him £1,000 – 'what a sum to pay for an encumbrance!' wrote his close friend, railway solicitor Francis Mewburn.

The bells are inscribed: 'Cast by John Warner & Son, London, 1863.' Mr Warner was a bellfounder from Norton-on-Tees who found fame in 1856 by volunteering to cast a bell for London that was so large it would become known as Big Ben.

The 7 foot diameter clock dials were to be illuminated by gas light. Unfortunately, on 26 September 1864, at 11 p.m., when men first tried to light the gas, they set fire to both the ladder they were standing on and the wooden floor. Spectators sent up buckets of water from the Tubwell Row fountain to dowse the fire.

'We also understand that the man who took the principal part in extinguishing the flames was burnt about the hands,' said the *D&ST*.

Originally, the clock face was red and the hands were golden. The naphtha gas, once they got it burning safely, burned green. The townspeople nicknamed the clock tower 'Dracula's Castle', and they struggled to see the time. Mr Pease agreed to further expenditure to make the dials white.

So by late 1864, the building was at last complete and in operation, even though the final cost to the board of £9,851 was well above Mr Waterhouse's £7,815 original estimate. Within two years, the board had to spend a further £2,615 boarding up the walls, to keep the factory pollution out, and adding canopies for additional stalls.

Plus Mr Pease had paid more than £1,000 from his own pocket, and an opponent on the board told him: 'You have spoiled the Market Place and you can't remedy it.'

The town's authorities faced another controversy: on market day, animals from far and wide still gormed unhygienically around the town centre. When a move to a cattle mart was proposed, publicans and shopkeepers got up a petition against it.

Nevertheless, on Monday 4 March 1878, a £14,000 mart, built on pastureland near Bank Top station, was formally opened. The *D&ST* said: 'The morning trains brought with them shoals of country folk on various errands bent; ruddy faced and long-coated dealers, plump and good tempered farmers' daughters, and those shabbiest of shabby men – the drovers.' Under the hammer that first morning were 11 bulls, 198 cows and heifers, 1,762 lean cattle, 115 pigs, 351 lean sheep and 60 fat sheep.

Nine hundred years of history had come to an end, and although there was considerable debate in the late twentieth and early twenty-first centuries about the cattle mart moving to an out-of-town location, the covered market has become the heartbeat of the town centre while Mr Pease's expensive encumbrance of a clock tower is the undisputed icon of Darlington.

An artist's impression of how the original clock looked: red face, gold numbers and a greenish hue. It was known as 'Dracula's Castle'.

The market complex makes a magnificent municipal statement that this is a town of some importance.

3. European Textile Centre

A 1907 postcard showing High Row with the coat of arms bottom right. In the centre is Backhouses' bank – the family started in the textile trade. The card was sent to Freda in Linthorpe from Bessie, who says: 'Just a pc to let you know how disappointed I was that I could not come to see you today. It has done nothing but rain in D'ton.'

Looking back at Hurworth from Low Hail bridge at the east end of the village. The riverside properties, many with rooms built into the rock, were all used by woollen workers.

In the centre of Darlington's old coat of arms there are three bales of wool – easily mistaken as barrels of beer – because, for centuries, Darlington's prosperity was built on textiles.

Wool led the way. In 1299, there's a mention of the monks of Durham priory buying Darlington-made 'bluett', which was a blue, woollen cloth.

Then plant-based linen, in which the yarn or material is spun from flax or hemp, rose in importance, as the rivers Skerne and Tees were found to have magical bleaching properties. As well as the earliest riverside properties on Northgate, the villages of Aycliffe, Hurworth and Neasham have bleaching beginnings. Daniel Defoe noted on his visit in the 1720s that 'the town is eminent for good bleaching of linen so that I have known cloth brought from Scotland to be bleached here'.

In the winter of 1745, the Duke of Cumberland, who was marching the king's army north to take on the Scots, camped thousands of men for five days on the Green Tree Fields behind Skinnergate. The townspeople noted that the men were 'lacking a sufficiency of creature-comforts', and so whistled up 10,000 flannel waistcoats to fit snugly under the soldiers' clothes and keep the belly and the breast warm.

Quality of clothing must, therefore, be a major reason why the king's army was able to defeat Bonnie Prince Charlie on the battlefield of Culloden, near Inverness, on 16 April 1746 – but even if the exact figure of 10,000 may be disputed, the anecdote shows how sizeable the linen industry was.

By the 1750s Darlington was 'the most noted place in the whole world for the linen manufacture of the sort called huckabacks ... great quantities of which are sent yearly to London, the broad sort being made nowhere else in England'. Huckaback was a coarse, absorbent linen made into tablecloths, napkins and tea towels – Darlington's greatest claim to fame was the size of its huckaback which was 'ten quarters wide'.

In the beginning, the products were created by piecework, a chain of private individuals passed a cloth from person to person, cottage to cottage, each performing a singular task upon it before handing it on. Gradually a handful of merchants emerged at the top of the pile, handing out the work and taking in the completed task, and following the flow of money.

At the top of the pile of linen were the Quaker Backhouse family, who began to industrialise the process by setting up a mill – known as either Low Mill or Bishop's Mill – on the opposite side of the Skerne to St Cuthbert's Church. Here they had a boil house and pegging posts, on which to dry the bleached linen.

The Darlington looms consumed so much flax that in the 1760s, an average of 207 tons of flax was imported into Stockton every year from the Baltic to supplement local production. In 1777, flax dealer John Clement, of High Row, took delivery of £500 worth of flax that had been grown in St Petersburg in Russia.

In 1787, the Backhouses financed one of their tenants in Low Mill, John Kendrew, as he invented and patented a spinning frame for hemp, tow, flax and wool. Three years later, their money enabled Kendrew to buy Darlington's first steam engine, from Boulton & Watt of Birmingham, which was installed in Low Mill and got the spinning frame spinning so well that Darlington became probably the largest producer of linen yarn in the country. The engine also allowed Kendrew to create a sideline of a spectacle-grinding mill in Low Mill. He sold his glasses across the north of England until unscrupulous entrepreneurs in Birmingham stole his unpatented idea and put it into mass production.

DID YOU KNOW?

In July 1838, twenty-year-old William Edward Forster became a 'gentleman apprentice' at Peases Mill. 'My occupation is woolsorting, under teaching of experienced North countrymen, gruffish, intelligent, in the main civil,' he wrote in his diary. 'Go to work at six; breakfast, eight; dine, half-past one; leave off six. An hour for breakfast, an hour and half for dinner. Employment dirty drudgery; standing tiring; bear it heroically because I hope it will do me good.' After a year, he gave up, became the Liberal MP for the textile town of Bradford, and his 1870 Education Act – 'the Forster Act' – allowed elementary schools to be set up on the rates by local councils for the first time.

As the eighteenth century drew to a close, the Backhouses realised banking could be more lucrative than linen making and so retreated to their counting house, leasing Low Mill to the other big Quaker textile family: the Peases.

The Peases were top of the pile of the woollen, or worsted, side of the industry. Their story starts when fourteen-year-old Edward Pease (1711–85) was sent from West Yorkshire on horseback with all his worldly possessions on his back to Darlington to shadow the wool-combing business of his uncle, Thomas Couldwell. Uncle Thomas had no children, and so when Edward married Elizabeth Coates in the Raby Meeting House in Staindrop on 7 July 1735, he started a dynasty that would dominate Darlington for the next 250 years.

In 1745, Uncle Thomas built offices on the Mill Holme, at the foot of Priestgate. Here the Skerne powered the Bishop of Durham's ancient corn mill, but Thomas was more interested in its potential for washing his wool and possibly driving his own mill.

Edward inherited the business in 1752, and took the sorting, combing, weaving and dyeing processes in-house on the Mill Holme. He followed the evolutionary path of the Backhouses, and with his eldest son, Joseph (1737–1808), set up a bank to control the flow of money through the production chain.

Their business prospered. By 1767, Joseph was living in one of the town centre's prime pieces of real estate, Bennett Hall (or The Grove, or just Peases House), which was off Bull Wynd, where his eldest son, Edward (1767–1858), was born – in this confusing family tree of identical names, this Edward would come to stand out as 'the Father of the Railways'.

But because he had yet to invent the railways, young Edward started his career on horseback, riding as far south as Lincolnshire, as far west as Carlisle and Penrith, and as far north as Edinburgh and Glasgow, buying fleeces to be spun in the Darlington mills, where the Peases had more than 1,000 looms under their control. They sent yarn as far afield as Exeter, where it was made into serges, and Stirling where it was turned into tartan, and in Darlington they made camblets, wildbores, bombazets, tammies and durants.

As the Peases flourished, they moved into one of the town centre's largest houses, in Bull Wynd, with Central Hall on the right.

Above left: Edward Pease might be known as the 'Father of the Railways' but he started out on horseback travelling the north of England buying fleeces.

Above right: Peases Mill seen from St Cuthbert's Church tower, in the 1920s, with the library and *The Northern Echo* offices behind.

An example of Edward's improving fortunes was that in 1798, newly married, he rented a substantial but plain house at the end of Northgate (which in 1821 would play a pivotal role in railway history). Within ten years, he could afford to buy it outright for £367 10s.

Henry Pease, who took charge of the mills when in his early twenties.

St Cuthbert's Church with Peases Mill behind on an Edwardian postcard.

Then came the Napoleonic Wars. As Quakers, the Peases were strict pacifists, against all wars, but they were also astute businessmen who made cloth and yarn for military uniforms. They did so well out of nearly fifteen years of fighting the French that by 1817, fifty-year-old Edward was considering retiring from the mill business.

On 2 February, a huge fire at the mill caused £30,000 of damage and put 600 people out of work. This gives some indication of the enormity of the Peases' business: £30,000 is worth more than £2.5 million today; 600 people were rendered unemployed out of a population of 6,551.

The Peases rebuilt, and Edward retired to go and invent the modern railway with George Stephenson. His youngest son, Henry, took charge of the mills, and in 1828, the twenty-one-year-old had 1,500 looms under his control and he employed a quarter of Darlington's male population, although mechanisation rapidly replaced the jobs for men, and by the middle of the century, the mill was primarily employing women and girls (boys got a look in as yarn winders).

In 1837, Henry built the Railway Mill near the Skerne railway bridge, off Northgate. Priestgate mills concentrated on yarn production, while the Railway, with its 400 looms, specialised in weaving and cloth production.

But trouble at the mills loomed. The textile trade required continuous investment and the Peases' minds were elsewhere. They wanted to play with their new trainsets; they wanted to live it up in their grand new mansions. They didn't want to fiddle around with old-fashioned mills.

In 1842, Edward wrote in his diary that he was giving 'serious consideration' with his sons to closing Priestgate, 'but', he concluded, 'the distress it would cause the poor, and the loss of £30,000 to £40,000 to the family, appear to render it prudent to try again'. Increasingly, as politics came to play a part in the Peases' fortune, the electoral consequences of throwing 1,000 or more town centre residents out of work were also a factor in the uneconomic equation.

DID YOU KNOW?
All Darlington revolved around the mill: from the middle of the seventeenth century, a bell was rung at 5.55 a.m., 8.25 a.m. and fifty-five minutes after midday to make sure the wool workers made it to work on time. If they were more than a quarter of an hour late, they had to enter the mill by the Penny Hole, in Priestgate, and pay a fine of 1d.

On the surface, the mills were greatly successful. All the flags that fluttered a welcome to the world's visitors to the 1851 Great Exhibition in London's Crystal Palace were made by the Peases in Priestgate. They won awards at exhibitions in America and Paris; the braid on the Prussian Guards' uniforms during the Franco-Prussian War of 1870–71 was made in the Peases' mills.

In the 1870s, the old Low Mill was closed and its 200 hands transferred to a new steam-powered mill on the north side of Priestgate. It was five storeys high, had seven boilers, a 250-horsepower engine and a 180 foot chimney, and it was formally opened on 28 December 1874, with all hands and their families attending a celebratory meal in Central Hall.

Yet, in reality, the mills were still not really profitable, particularly not in a time of economic depression. In 1882, Alfred Pease argued passionately for the closure of 'this dreadful sink which swallows up an overdraft of £7,000-a-year'.

Still, at an exhibition in Bradford in 1882, Darlington cloth won the Gold Medal of the Clothworkers' Company of the City of London, and the Peases had the honour of manufacturing dress material for Princess Alexandra, the future queen.

With losses mounting, in 1884, the Peases called in outside help. They remained as directors, but leased the mills to Edward Clarke, of Ripon, and William Smith, of Helensburgh, near Glasgow.

The new management did not bring about a change of fortune, and in 1891, the Railway Mill was closed, bringing weaving in the town to an end (its chimney survived until 1948).

Even worse, at 11.45 a.m. on Monday 26 February 1894, 'one of the most disastrous fires that Darlington has ever witnessed' broke out in the Priestgate mill's old engine room, in the south side of the complex near the River Skerne.

'Thick black volumes of smoke poured from the shattered windows and doorways,' reported *The Northern Echo*.

Fortunately, the 6 a.m. shift was on its lunch break, so many of the girls were either out or on the move. Still, 614 of them lost their shawls and boots in the blaze. Some girls, though, were stranded on the top storey with the staircases filling up with blinding, choking smoke.

They clambered out of the upper floor windows and crept 'along a narrow stone parapet at the top of the building' to where overlooker William Langhorne tied ropes around their waists and lowered them on to the single-storey roofs beneath.

'Willing hands on the lower roof caught them as they came within reach,' said the *Echo*. 'Several of the girls fainted away in the arms of the policemen.'

Next morning, even while the south side smouldered, the north side workers were trooping into the mill. They, though, were probably the fortunate ones because 400 of the south side girls lost their jobs, and a Mayor's Relief Fund was set up to assist them.

It cost £80,000 to rebuild, but continued to be such a drain on the family finances – between 1871 and 1902, it lost £260,477 (around £31 million in today's values) – that it was a major contributory factor in the Peases' spectacular financial collapse of 1902. Lister & Company, of Manningham, Bradford, took over and managed the mill's slow decline – and a third major mill fire, this time in the northern mill on Sunday 2 July 1933. It was the hottest day of the year – '88 in the shade in Darlington' – and it was believed that the sun's rays beaming into the wool warehouse set alight some clippings.

The alarm was again raised at 11.45 a.m., and twenty-two firemen were quickly on the scene, but 'it was unfortunate that the brigade's biggest engine, No 1, is at present away being repainted and having pneumatic tyres fitted', noted the *Echo*.

Peases Mill seen from *The Northern Echo* offices in the 1950s.

A rare colour photo of Peases Mill in 1982 shortly before it was demolished. (Picture: Mick Harris)

Unfortunate was an understatement. This was probably the biggest blaze of the twentieth century in Darlington and the engine was away for a paint job! But at least the firemen managed to rescue the mill cat, Jinnie, although her unnamed kitten was lost.

The Second World War perked the mill up a bit – Priestgate made enough thread for battledress to stretch 300 times around the world – but peacetime saw a steady decline. In 1964, the warehouses behind the library were demolished and replaced by a discotheque and bowling alley, and in 1966, Lister began investing £3 million in its Barrow business, where it employed 1,000 people as opposed to Darlington's 400.

> DID YOU KNOW?
> Skinnergate was established in the mid-fourteenth century in testimony to the street's leatherworkers, but by the sixteenth century, they had moved to the Clay Row, east of the River Skerne, in search of water and lime. By the seventeenth century, leather may have been the town's most significant industry, and by the mid-nineteenth century, where the inner ring road is today, there were numerous lime pits, bark letches and urine cisterns, mainly controlled by the Middleton family. In 1892, with the industry finished, streets – including Middleton Street – were laid across their works, although it wasn't until 1901 that washing an animal skin in the Skerne was officially declared a public nuisance and so banned.

The writing was on the wall, and the weaving on the loom, in 1970 when Priestgate's most sophisticated equipment, which created man-made fibres, was transferred across the Pennines. Finally, in 1972, strikes caused power cuts that emboldened the management enough to lay off the remaining seventy-five female workers. When the lights came back on a month or so later, Peases Mill remained in darkness, never to operate again.

The ugly hulk of a mill was demolished in the early 1980s, and its site became a scratty car park until the Sports Direct superstore and multistorey car park was built at the start of the twenty-first century, so obliterating the last traces of the industry on which Darlington's prosperity, the world's railways and the town's coat of arms, was based.

There's no sign of Peases Mill today – it is the site of a Sports Direct outlet.

4. Global Railway Centre

Edward Pease, the 'Father of the Railways'.

Edward Pease's house is now two kebab takeaways and a Domino's pizza parlour.

On the evening of 19 April 1821, two strangers approached the front door of Edward Pease's home in Northgate, which is now a kebab takeaway and a pizza parlour.

Mr Pease headed his family's traditional woollen interests, which had enjoyed fifteen years of profits making uniforms for the Napoleonic Wars, but his family had always been aware of a coming new age. In 1767, his grandfather, also Edward, had attended a meeting in the Posthouse, in Post House Wynd, which had discussed the possibility of connecting the south Durham coalfield with a seaport on the Tees at Stockton by canal. That meeting had instructed the foremost canal builder of the day, James Brindley, to draw up the Winston to Stockton canal plan, which imagined docks in Cockerton and a basin near Skinnergate. Donors to the scheme had included five Peases and two Backhouses, but eventually, the canal had been holed below the waterline by a lack of finance.

Yet the idea was watertight. Every generation revived it, and in the years after the Napoleonic Wars, the Peases and Backhouses had their own fortunes and were able to tap into a national network of Quakers. Aided by a committee of railway pioneers, they approached Parliament for permission to build their line.

Jonathan Backhouse, of Polam Hall, also brought bravery to the railway table. The early plans had the trackbed going across land at Summerhouse, Ingleton and Hilton which was owned by the Earl of Darlington, of Raby Castle. His lordship lived for fox hunting, and the line was proposed to go through one of his fox coverts – an artificial earth that more or less guaranteed that there was always a fox to chase whenever his lordship fancied a hunt.

The earl, William Harry Vane, was outraged and so he determined to derail the railway. First of all, he tried Parliamentary means, but then turned to underhand monetary measures. In those days, you were able to take a one pound banknote into a bank and demand a pound of gold in return. The earl ordered all of his Teesdale tenants to secretly save Backhouses' banknotes so that he could, unannounced, present a vast number to the bank on High Row (where Barclays is today) and demand that they all be turned into bullion, knowing full well that Backhouses would not have enough in their vaults. The bank would become bankrupt, the railway it was bankrolling would collapse, and his foxes could relax in his coverts until he wanted to chase them...

In late June 1819, Mr Backhouse got wind of the plan and dashed down the Great North Road in his carriage pulled by four horses. He went round the friendly Quaker banks, borrowing as much bullion as possible and loading it in his carriage, and then he dashed back up the Great North Road.

But having been away from home for ninety-six hours, when he reached Croft bridge – just three miles from Darlington – one of the four wheels came crashing off his wagon, and he ground to an agonising halt, unable to move.

Meanwhile, the earl's agent was in Darlington, with months and months of banknotes in his bag, on his way to 'break Backhouses'.

Jonathan Backhouse, the head banker who balanced the cash. (Picture courtesy of Darlington Centre for Local Studies)

Backhouses Bank has been at the centre of High Row for more than 200 years, although its premises in 1821 were as this early 1860s photo shows. (Picture courtesy of Darlington Centre for Local Studies)

Jonathan was a resourceful fellow. He took all the bullion off the broken front axle and piled it onto the good rear wheels, causing the broken axle to lift up off the ground. And so, pulling a wheelie, he dashed the remaining miles into High Row – apparently welcomed into town by cheering people.

Breathless, he was at his counter when the earl's agent arrived, and he calmly cashed all the notes. He even had a pile of gold leftover, and as the agent departed, he politely added: 'Now, tell thy master that if he will sell Raby, I will pay for it in the same metal.'

So, the dastardly lord was thwarted. There is a wonderful painting of the incident, created sixty years later by Backhouses employee and renowned Darlington artist Samuel Tuke Richardson. Backhouses' books still survive. The entries are written in the simple Quaker style, which calls months by their numbers rather than their names (which are usually derived from ancient, false gods): '1819, 6th month, 25th. To bank and cash to London £32,000'

According to the Bank of England's Inflation Calculator, in today's values, Jonathan had around £2.75 million of gold in his carriage as he dashed up the Great North Road, dodging the highwaymen of the day.

The next entry in the bank's loss account reads: '1819, 7th month, 31st. Wheel demolished. £2 3s 0d.'

So, for a couple of quid, the fox-hunting Lord Darlington was foiled, and the Stockton & Darlington Railway was saved.

And the worst pun in local history was born, because, on Croft bridge, the way the gold was moved off the broken front axle onto the good rear one causing the broken axle to be lifted off the ground is known as how Jonathan Backhouse balanced the cash!

Because of Mr Backhouse's bravery and the enormity of Mr Pease's bank account, the pioneers pushed their bill through Parliament, and on the evening of 19 April 1821, Mr Pease was at home anxiously awaiting news from London where George IV was due that day to give it royal assent.

As he waited, two strangers approached his front door, unannounced. They came from wildest Northumberland and had set off early that morning by horse for Newcastle. At Newcastle, they caught a stagecoach bound for Stockton 'by nip' – tipping the driver rather than paying the fare. From Stockton, they walked 12 miles across farm and field, following the path that was proposed for the Stockton & Darlington Railway – this was their way of doing fieldwork.

One version of the story says they 'walked barefoot to Darlington, shoeing themselves near the Bulmer Stone' before crossing the road to Mr Pease's home.

Barefoot would have saved their shoe leather, although another version of the story has them stopping at the stone to take their shoes off in deference to the great Quaker entrepreneur they were approaching.

In 1899, Backhouses merged with Barclays, but the branch is in the same place on High Row as it was in Jonathan Backhouse's day.

How Jonathan Backhouse balanced the cash, as seen by bank employee Samuel Tuke Richardson in 1875. (Picture courtesy of Barclays Group Archives)

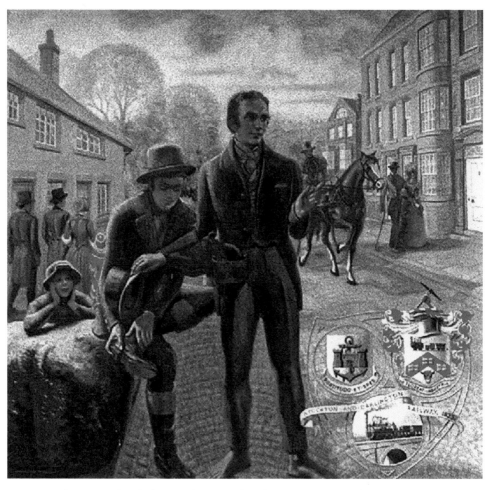

George Stephenson and Nicholas Wood sort out their footware on Bulmer's Stone, opposite Edward Pease's house, on 19 April 1821. (Picture courtesy of Darlington Centre for Local Studies)

The original badge of the Stockton & Darlington Railway was drawn in early 1821 and shows the company was still expecting horses to be the motive force, which is why the meeting of 19 April 1821 was so revolutionary.

In stockings or shoes it matters not: as they didn't have an appointment, Edward's butler turned them away. Edward, ears a-flapping upstairs, came rushing down to sort out the commotion and ushered them into the kitchen – now the kebab takeaway part of the complex – where he learned that they were Nicholas Wood, the viewer (manager) of Killingworth Colliery, and George Stephenson, the colliery engineer.

DID YOU KNOW?
The Skerne Bridge was the largest piece of infrastructure on the Stockton & Darlington Railway. George Stephenson was commissioned to build it in 1824, but when he ran into problems with the foundations, the railway committee ordered him to take advice from Ignatius Bonomi, the Durham county bridge surveyor. On 6 July 1824, Francis Mewburn, the world's first railway solicitor, laid the foundation stone for the bridge designed by Bonomi, the first railway architect.

It was here that Stephenson convinced Pease that the railway should be operated by new-fangled steam locomotive rather than pulled by old-fashioned horses. There is a lot of romantic elaboration surrounding this meeting, but its conclusions changed the world – and put Darlington at the head and centre of the railway revolution. Pease engaged Stephenson as his engineer, and slowly, the 26-mile track crept across the countryside. He also set Stephenson's son, Robert, up in business in Newcastle to build the first engine – *Locomotion No. 1* – for the line.

A cigarette card showing The Experiment, the world's first passenger carriage, as made for the opening day of the S&DR.

Isaac Pease's headstone in the Quaker cemetery behind Skinnergate says that he died on '9th month 27th 1825' – 27 September 1825 was the opening day of the Stockton & Darlington Railway.

It all came together on Tuesday 27 September 1825. The first wagons containing coal and flour were lowered from Witton Park down the Etherley Incline by a stationary engine. They crossed the Gaunless by horsepower and were then pulled up Brusselton Incline by a second stationary engine on the top. Finally, with hundreds of people clinging to the sides, they were lowered 880 yards down to the Masons' Arms where, at 8 a.m., *Locomotion No. 1* was steaming in readiness.

Three hundred people had told the pioneers that they wanted tickets for the inaugural journey, but at least 600 people charged at the trucks determined to hitch a ride. The committee members took their places in The Experiment, the world's first passenger railway coach, which seated eighteen people across an aisle.

Sadly, Edward Pease was not among them. That very morning, his son, twenty-two-year-old Isaac, died in the family home in Northgate, Darlington. 'Isaac had always been a delicate boy, and the fond heart of the old man had gone out towards the weakly member of his numerous household,' reported *The Northern Echo* in 1875. 'Edward Pease had always said that none of his children were so gifted as Isaac.'

In that first train, there were about thirty-eight items. *Locomotion* and its tender were followed by five wagons full of coal and passengers, one wagon of flour and passengers, one wagon of surveyors and engineers, The Experiment, six wagons of seated people, fourteen wagons of standing workmen and six wagons of coal and passengers.

The railway workmen wore blue buttonholes and the railwaymen on duty wore blue sashes. These men stood on the couplings between wagons ready to apply the brakes.

Timothy Hackworth was the guard, and George Stephenson and his brothers James and Ralph were in charge of the engine. At 10 a.m., Hackworth gave the signal and the inaugural train moved off.

'The welkin rang with loud huzzas, while the happy faces of some, the vacant stares of others, and the alarm depicted on the countenances of not a few, gave variety to the picture,' recalled a witness.

Soon, *Locomotion* was pulling its 80-ton train and its 553 passengers at a speed of 8 miles per hour. Dozens of horse-drawn coaches in its wake struggled to keep up. Near Aycliffe, one of the wagons came off the line, and a bystander, John Davison, was struck but not badly injured. At Simpasture, *Locomotion No. 1* lost power, and George Stephenson had to work for thirty-five minutes to clear a blockage in a pipe, but by the time they rattled across Aycliffe Lane level crossing (now Heighington station), the train was charging along at 15 mph.

The train arrived in north Darlington at midday. It had taken two hours to cover 9 miles, with three stoppages totalling fifty-five minutes, and so its average speed was 8 mph. George Stephenson refilled its large wooden water barrel in the tender – a barrel so large that the cooper, Mason Brotherton, was forced to assemble it outside his workshop, in Blackwellgate, Darlington.

During the thirty-minute break, six wagonloads of coal were distributed to the poor people of Darlington, and a couple of hundred railway workmen were despatched to the town's pubs for free food and beer. The Yarm Band took the place of distributed coal in the train and prepared to 'oompah' the 12 miles to Stockton.

Locomotion No. 1 on display at Bank Top station. It became the centrepiece of the railway museum in North Road when that opened in 1975.

The Skerne Bridge was the largest piece of infrastructure on the Stockton & Darlington Railway of 1825.

On the opening day, *Locomotion No. 1* stopped at the crossing where the railway went over the Great North Road to the north of Darlington. In 1827, a shed was erected on this intersection for passengers to shelter in, and in 1842, North Road station – now a museum – was completed.

When the train left North Road at 12.30 p.m., a man, John Dixon after whom there is a street named in Darlington, was riding on horseback ahead of it carrying a red flag. There were probably around 700 people onboard – a majority of them clinging to the sides of the coal wagons – as it went over the Skerne Bridge, the largest piece of infrastructure on the line.

Inevitably, an accident happened. John Stevens, a keelman who had attached himself to the wagon in front of the railway pioneers in The Experiment coach, lost his fingerhold. He tumbled down and the wagons ran over his foot, crushing it horribly. The last mention that history affords Mr Stevens is that medical men said an amputation was the only way to save his life. It is not recorded if it did.

The line curved south through Fighting Cocks and Middleton St George to Goosepool, where Stephenson again stopped to replenish the water barrel. At Preston Park, *Locomotion No 1* (passengers 700, horses nil) drew alongside a stagecoach (passengers sixteen, horses four). For a while, they were neck and neck at 15 mph, but quickly *Locomotion* ran out the winner as the horses tired.

Its victory lap led it into Stockton at 3.45 p.m. where, at the company's wharf beside the River Tees, a twenty-one-gun salute greeted its arrival. It had taken the locomotive five hours and forty-five minutes to cover the 20 miles from Shildon. The celebrations lasted until it was dark and late, and when the pioneers returned to their railway for a ride home, they found it had been vandalised with tree trunks by those who wished it to fail.

DID YOU KNOW?
Another surviving piece of substantial infrastructure from the opening day of the S&DR is the 'accommodation tunnel' off Arnold Road. It doesn't really have a name, and the new Eastern Transport Corridor flies over the top of it, but it was built around 1824, probably to George Stephenson's design, to allow a farmer at Hundens to get his cattle underneath the tracks without them being squashed – it accommodated the needs of the farmer.

It would be several years before Timothy Hackworth's engineering skills made steam power a revolutionary success as a mode of transport, but it was Darlington money, ingenuity, bravery and far-sightedness that established the world's first modern railway – with what is now a kebab takeaway playing a vital role in this story of global significance. Fortunately, when the first coat of arms was essayed in 1868, a kebab was a culinary experience yet to be enjoyed in Darlington, otherwise it might have been included!

5. Scandals

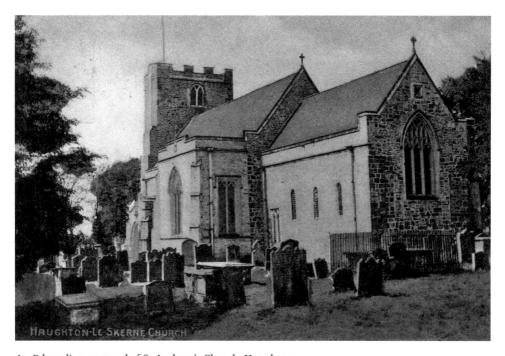

An Edwardian postcard of St Andrew's Church, Haughton.

The Cheese Affair

By an accident of history, the vicar of Haughton-le-Skerne was an extremely wealthy man. In 1861, his salary was £1,300 a year (£150,000 in today's money, according to the Bank of England's inflation calculator). By contrast, to the west of the Skerne in Darlington, the three vicars were paid only £600 between them.

The post was highly prized. Great men were appointed to it, men so great that they rarely deigned to visit the flock they were supposed to be tending. For example, Dr Bulkeley Bandinel was said to have 'held it since 1822 without letting it interfere in any way with his more important responsibilities as librarian of the Bodleian at Oxford'.

In his absence, Haughton was run by a curate, Revd R. J. Simpson, who, in 1860, asked Robert Waistell to move from the pew he had occupied every Sunday for seventy-three years. Mr Waistell used unholy language towards the curate, and the bitter row spilled out into the streets and onto the pages of the local newspapers. Eventually, the curate prevailed, but God moves in mysterious ways...

THE DURHAM CHEESE
Bishop (to Needy Clergyman).—"I am exceedingly sorry, dear brother in the church, but you see I have not a drop left for you. I have poured it all into my cheese."

Above left: Revd Edward Cheese, the vicar of Haughton from 1861 to 1886.

Above right: A later reproduction of the *Punch* cartoon that lampooned the Bishop of Durham for creating a stink in Haughton over cheese.

The following year, Dr Bandinel retired to spend more time with his books. It fell to the newly enthroned Bishop of Durham, Rt Revd Henry Montagu Villiers, to appoint his successor.

For the people of Darlington, this represented an opportunity to redress the balance. The three vicars in Darlington who rushed around ministering to more than 15,000 people together earned less than half the expensive vicar in Haughton, who only had 1,000 in his congregation.

However, Bishop Villiers rejected their pleas. He said that he had a candidate in mind who would be worth his salt. In February 1861, he announced the identity of the new rector: Revd Edward Cheese. Aged twenty-eight, Mr Cheese had been in holy orders for only three years and just happened to be the bishop's son-in-law, married for only a few months to his eldest daughter, Amy Maria.

DID YOU KNOW?
St Andrew's Church in Haughton-le-Skerne is, perhaps surprisingly, Darlington's oldest church. It was started around 1125 whereas Bishop Hugh de Puiset didn't get round to commencing work on St Cuthbert's, in the town centre, until the 1180s. Both churches, though, are probably on the sites of earlier Saxon chapels.

At a time when members of the clergy were unpopular due to their extravagant lifestyles, the appointment of Mr Cheese stank to high heaven. The *Darlington Telegraph* – a Conservative paper that was supportive of the bishop – said the announcement was made 'to the chagrin of the petitioners and the excitement in the public mind'. The *Manchester Guardian* accused the bishop of 'gross nepotism'.

Punch magazine took up the cause, and for all four of its weekly issues in March 1861, it pilloried the bishop with bad fromage-related puns. Under the heading 'Crème de la crème', it said: 'It is quite a mistake to suppose that the Rev Edward Cheese is of humble origin. We are assured that he is of a very old family in Cheshire.' Then it broke into poetry:

> To your CHEESE'S merits you'll find a blindness –
> There'll be a bishopped flavour to him, –
> Be he made of the milk of human kindness,
> Or the sourest and smallest sectarian skim.
> This moral for all sucking clergy I draw,
> Beware of Episcopal fathers-in-law!
> Here's one who to heart that moral should lay;
> He'll not find Haughton a chapel-of-ease,
> And be he what he may, the public will say,
> That your conduct is anything but the Cheese.
> In case its readers didn't get all of the gags, Punch added a footnote: 'In the diocese of
> Durham boiled milk, which has been allowed to burn, is said to be 'bishoppped'

A full-page cartoon, showing the bishop decanting a £1,300 bottle of port into a Stilton cheese while refusing to give any money to a needy clergyman, was said to have hit Mr Villiers hard. He talked of resigning, but his friends urged him to stay on. The strain of the national opprobrium, though, affected his health, and he died at Auckland Castle after a fortnight's illness on 9 August 1861, aged forty-eight.

However, in Haughton Mr Cheese proved to be a breath of fresh air. He sacked the hated curate and, unlike the previous incumbent, resided in the village and worked hard among his people. He, too, died young, aged only fifty-one in 1886, but his wife, Mrs Cheese, lived on to 1934, dying at a ripe old age.

Chinese Sex Scandal

The Backhouses were the epitome of trustworthiness and dependability. It was on their credit that a century of railways, coal mines and ships in County Durham was built. It is their Gothic headquarters that dominates High Row, and it was their head banker, Edmund Backhouse, who became Darlington's first MP in 1868.

And it is Edmund's grandson who was the Backhouses' blackest sheep and Darlington's darkest horse who enjoyed having his bare bottom beaten with an ivory fan during mammoth sex sessions with the voracious Chinese Empress, T'zu-his.

Above left: Sir Edmund Backhouse, the 'hermit of Peking' and, from 1918, the 2nd Baronet of Uplands in Darlington.

Above right: Sir Jonathan Edmund Backhouse, the 1st Baronet of Uplands and father of the fantasist Sir Edmund.

Looking south at the Hummersknott mansion, which is now at the centre of Carmel College. Behind it is Uplands.

Edmund's son was Jonathan Edmund Backhouse who, in 1901, was created a baronet for his services to the Liberal Unionist Party. He chose as his title the name of his mansion, Uplands, which was near today's Hummersknott School.

His son, Edmund Trelawny Backhouse, was born in 1873 at The Rookery in Middleton Tyas, the family's country retreat. Young Edmund was packed off to boarding school in Ascot by the age of nine, and then went to Oxford University, where he showed enormous potential as both a linguist and a fantasist – he claimed to be fluent in forty-eight languages, which may well have been true, but his close friendship with Winston Churchill, and his homosexual affairs with Oscar Wilde and Lord Rosebery, who later became prime minister, were made up.

More worrying to the banking Backhouses was that Edmund had amassed £23,000 of debts (around £2.5 million in today's values) and was facing bankruptcy. His father finessed the embarrassment away and spirited Edmund out of the country to distant China, which was then closed to the West.

His linguist brilliance opened doors in the highest places. He was made a professor at Peking University and used his inside track to write exclusive articles for *The Times*. As his was the only voice from inside China, these articles dictated Western governments' policies.

As the Qing dynasty faded away, China slipped into the Boxer Rebellion and Edmund took up arms – although his Darlington relatives reckoned he managed only to shoot his own sergeant-major.

Amid the rubble of the revolution, Edmund discovered a treasure trove of documents, which he sent back to the Bodleian Museum at Oxford University, and the diaries of His Excellency Ching-shan, which he used as the basis of his revelatory book about the end of the dynasty, a book he may have part written when visiting Darlington and Tyas in 1910. This book, *China Under the Empress Dowager*, secured his reputation as the finest sinologist of his day.

Back in China in 1915, Edmund promised Lord Kitchener, the Secretary of State for War, that he had acquired from revolutionaries a huge consignment of leftover armaments. He claimed he had 200,000 rifles, 30 million rounds of ammunition and 350 machine guns sailing discretely down the Yang-tse Kiang River. A delighted Kitchener, desperate for weaponry, left Edmund £2 million in a dead-letter box in Hong Kong, but the flotilla never arrived. It never existed. It was a figment of Edmund's imagination.

Edmund's reputation began to fade, particularly when suggestions arose that the diaries on which his book had been based were also fake.

On his father's death in 1918, he became the 2nd Baronet of Uplands in Darlington, but he buried himself deep in China, becoming known as the 'hermit of Peking' and writing up his tall tales until his death in 1944.

When his biographer, Trevor-Roper, looked at the tall tales in the 1970s, he concluded that Sir Edmund was a forger, a fraud and a lurid fantasist, a conclusion that was borne out when the last of Sir Edmund's manuscripts was published in 2011 to global astonishment.

> DID YOU KNOW?
> Uplands and Hummersknott were sister mansions, designed by Alfred Waterhouse
> in the mid-1860s. The architect, who became one of the greatest of his generation,
> was also building the covered market complex, Rockliffe Hall at Hurworth,
> and Backhouses bank on High Row at the same time. Hummersknott was built
> for Alfred Pease, son of Joseph, whereas Uplands was for Alfred's sister, Rachel.
> Hummersknott is now at the centre of Carmel College, but Uplands, which was
> taken over during the Second World War by the Crown Film Unit and a camouflage
> school, was demolished in the early 1970s.

The book, *Decadence Mandchoue*, opens in 1898 when twenty-five-year-old Edmund entered the House of Chaste Pleasures, was washed and perfumed by eunuchs, and was called to the bedchamber of the sixty-nine-year-old dowager empress. Their love-making sessions were extended by her secret recipe of bird's nest soup, and so hot did they become that they had to be cooled by electric fans blowing over large blocks of ice.

It carried on for ten years, until the seventy-nine-year-old empress, who had ruled China for forty-nine years, passed away – not through exhaustion, said Sir Edmund, but because she was assassinated by a warlord. That, too, was fantasy. The empress really died of dysentery after eating over-ripe figs.

You cannot believe a word written by the 2nd Baron of Uplands. As if to eradicate him from the town's memory, the 1860s mansion after which he was named was demolished in the 1970s.

Political Scandal

Ignatius Timothy Trebitsch-Lincoln, the MP for Darlington who is the greatest parliamentary scandal of the twentieth century.

A *Punch* cartoon showing the Darlington MP Trebitsch-Lincoln holding forth on behalf of his constituents in 1910.

Darlington has obliterated Trebitsch-Lincoln's memory: his home, Park View, has been replaced by a petrol station.

Timothy Ignatius Trebitsch Lincoln was a conman, thief, spy, double agent, Christian missionary, fraudster, Buddhist monk and an adulterer. He was also the Member of Parliament for Darlington for eleven months in 1910 and so must be the only person ever to hold positions in both the British and German legislatures.

He was born in 1879 in Budapest in Hungary, which he had to flee when he was eighteen due to allegations of stolen gold watches. He briefly became an Anglican missionary in Canada and a curate in Kent, and then, following a chance meeting on a train, he inveigled his way into the life of Benjamin Seebohm Rowntree, the millionaire philanthropist from the York chocolate firm, who sponsored him to tour Europe researching a book about Liberal social policy.

After a couple of years of embarrassing scrapes that nearly became international incidents, the book was complete and Rowntree assisted Trebitsch's selection as the Liberal parliamentary candidate for Darlington, where the Rowntree family co-owned a newspaper called *The Northern Echo*.

Darlington, though, was a Pease seat. The Peases had been Liberal in the distant past, but at the opening of the twentieth century, they'd turned Tory – the mill girls in Priestgate reputedly wore red knickers on election day as that was the local Conservative colour.

So Trebitsch faced an uphill battle. He arrived in town in April 1909, installing his family in Park View, Grange Road, a substantial residence overlooking South Park. He adorned every room with a picture of his new hero, Abraham Lincoln, whose surname he adopted as his own.

The townspeople, though, were suspicious of this imposed foreigner – he was still a Hungarian citizen. His wife, Margarathe, later wrote: 'We had the unpleasant experience of being pelted by our opponents with banana skins, stones wrapped in paper, and rotten eggs.'

However, he turned his foreignness into an attribute. 'You are Britishers by the mere accident of birth,' he told them in his thick accent. 'I am a Britisher by choice.' He also campaigned on a great British theme, their love of animals, claiming that the protectionism of Herbert Pike Pease, the sitting MP, was making the German working men so poor that they had to eat horses and pet dogs.

Around 95 per cent of the all-male electorate voted on 15 January 1910, and after a recount, the result was projected at 10.30 p.m. onto a large screen in a crowded Market Place, outside the old town hall: Lincoln I. T. T. (Liberal) 4,815; Pease, H. Pike (Unionist) 4,786 – against the odds, Trebitsch had secured a majority of twenty-nine.

The 1910 parliament was the second shortest of the twentieth century, and by the time it collapsed in December, police forces in Hungary, Romania and Germany were after him, and the Austrian government was enraged by a speech he'd made in the Commons. The Darlington electorate by now knew he was a conman and the Rowntrees had discovered he owed them around £10,000 short. With debts crowding in on him, Trebitsch withdrew a week before polling day and slunk out of town, never to return.

At the outbreak of the First World War, he was censor at a London mail sorting office, but he was sacked for writing on the letters. Desperate for money, he tried to sell the British War Office a plan he had concocted to destroy the German Navy. When the British refused to entertain him, he slipped over the Channel to German-occupied Rotterdam and tried to sell the enemy the same plan. Initially, the Germans were very interested in this former MP turned turncoat, but after a month they realised he was a charlatan.

By now, half of Europe's police officers were after him for everything from high treason to low pilfering. So, on 30 January 1915, Trebitsch said farewell to his wife and sons (one of whom was later executed for murder) and sailed for America. On the voyage, he met and made love to a married woman and her younger sister.

In May in New York, he sold his fantastically exaggerated life story to *The World* magazine, who splashed it in big headlines: 'Revelations of ITT Lincoln, Former Member of Parliament Who Became a German Spy. Amazing confession of a naturalised subject of England who, for revenge, sought to betray his adopted country to her enemies.'

After leading American and British police a merry dance, he was extradited and sentenced to three years in prison for fraud. He was released in 1919 and deported, but ended up in Germany in league with right-wing revolutionaries led by Dr Wolfgang Kapp, plotting to overthrow the Weimar Republic. With incredulity, the *Echo* reported him to be conducting negotiations with the deposed kaiser, and then, when the revolution was successful, that Dr Kapp had made him the press spokesman for the new German government.

When the *Daily Telegraph*'s Berlin correspondent asked the new administration for a statement about its relations with Britain, the former MP for Darlington appeared to present it. 'There is something almost Olympian about this man's scoundrelism,' said the newspaper in flabbergasted amazement in March 1920.

The Kapp government lasted just five days and on 6 June 1921, after a week in an Austrian prison, Trebitsch announced enigmatically: 'My destination is a profound secret. I shall disappear as if the earth had swallowed me up and I shall reappear in an unexpected quarter within eight years. Meanwhile, I shall accomplish my task.'

He duly reappeared in a most unexpected quarter – China – where he was advising various brutal warlords on improving their relations with Europe. This involved him travelling a lot and having sexual relations with women who were not his wife. He then turned to religion and became a Buddhist monk.

'I made the great renunciation,' he trumpeted. 'I quitted the world. I forced the doors of the lunatic asylum open and walked out.'

He called himself The Venerable Chao Kung and set himself up in China with thirteen disciples, who signed over all their worldly goods to him and followed him slavishly around the world as he tried 'to rescue the multitudes' through his preaching.

On 6 May 1934, they arrived to astonishment in Liverpool, shaven-headed in grey kimonos and black skull caps. Trebitsch was arrested and dragged off to jail with one of his nuns clinging tearfully to the side of the truck. He spent five days inside before being deported once more. His penniless disciples began deserting him, the final straw for one monk being when he found 'the abbot' in 'an embarrassing position' with one of the young nuns.

And so he died alone on 6 October 1943, in Shanghai General Hospital. Officially, he passed away during an intestinal operation, but there is a theory that his stomach had been eaten away by poison administered to him by the local branch of the Nazi Gestapo on the personal orders of Adolf Hitler, who was fed up with the constant crazed letter writing of the former MP for Darlington.

Royal Scandal

Above left: Revd R. A. Jardine with Lord Louis Mountbatten at the chateau in Tours.

Above right: St Paul's Church in Northgate was packed in 1937 to witness the controversial cleric in matrimonial action.

The site of St Paul's Church today, although the vicarage still stands in the middle of a housing association's properties.

NORTHERN DESPATCH, THURSDAY, 3 JUNE, 1937

FAME AT LAST

Yesterday Darlington meant nothing to the world—but today, thanks to the Rev. R. A. Jardine, we're famous.

How the *Evening Despatch* showed that Revd R. A. Jardine had put Darlington at the centre of a world sensation.

On Sunday 30 May 1937, a few minutes before Evensong at St Paul's Church in Darlington, Revd Robert Anderson Jardine received a telegram that put him on edge.

Evensong sung, he and his wife, Maud, hurried away from the North Road church and disappeared from town. On Tuesday 1 June a rumour whistled round Darlington that he had arrived at a chateau in France where he was apparently going to marry the ex-king Edward VIII, now known as the Duke of Windsor, and his twice-divorced American lover, Wallis Simpson.

'The news has come as a complete surprise to Darlington people,' said the now-defunct *Evening Despatch*. 'Mr Jardine has been in Darlington for ten years, and is well known for his unusual views.'

His unusual view in this case was that no one should be denied a Church of England blessing – no one, not even the prince who had abdicated from the British throne for love – and he had telegrammed as much to the Chateau de Cande, near Tours, where the royal couple had gone to escape the furore of the greatest royal scandal of the twentieth century. They'd telegrammed him back, asking him to pop over immediately, and so, on Thursday 3 June, the railwaymen's vicar from Darlington – he was nicknamed the 'poor man's parson' by the press – officiated at the most controversial of royal weddings. It took him just twenty minutes.

The duchess gave him a slice of cake to take home; the duke gave him a pair of inscribed cufflinks and a glass of champagne. Then he was off, the duke shouting 'Goodbye Jardine' as he left the chateau to motor through the night back to Darlington.

'Pressmen, photographers and cameramen were after us like wild dogs, but we gave them the slip,' he said later.

They were waiting for him at St Paul's Church on the morning of Saturday, 5 June where he was to marry George Gamble and Doris Haylett. Seven hundred were crammed inside the church and hundreds more – including TV cameramen from America – lined North Road, hoping to get a glimpse of the controversial cleric in matrimonial action.

At the end of the service, he told the new Mr and Mrs Gamble: 'I shall now put this book away and it will not be used any more after today. You have had exactly the same service, word for word, as the duke and duchess at the chateau.' He gave them his slice of wedding cake before retiring to his rectory to read the 4,000 letters and telegrams that had arrived in his absence (all but four were supportive, he claimed).

A fortnight later, he announced from his pulpit that he was resigning and he and Maud immediately embarked for America on the *Queen Mary* liner for a lecture tour, where he was billed as 'the Duke's vicar'.

He lived out the last twelve years of his life in Texas, still coloured by controversy. American bishops boycotted him and accused him of being a fame-hungry mercenary. He, though, just loved to talk about his involvement in what he called 'the greatest romance that has ever taken place'.

His church, beside Northlands Methodist church, burned down in 1973 and has been replaced by flats, although his rectory still stands.

6. War Heroes

Michael 'Spud' Murphy

Michael 'Spud' Murphy, the only Victoria Cross winner to be buried in Darlington, and one of only eight buried in County Durham.

In 1891, Michael Murphy was living in Wilton Lodge, then a one-bedroom property in the countryside. Now it is a three-bedroom home at the top of Nunnery Lane.

Michael Murphy is buried in North Cemetery beneath a headstone paid for by his benefactor, Sir Henry Havelock-Allan of Blackwell Grange.

The only Victoria Cross winner to be buried in Darlington is Michael 'Spud' Murphy, an Irishman who is a long way from home – he was born in Tipperary in 1831 (although his headstone in North Cemetery says 1832). He was a blacksmith by trade, and enlisted as a farrier in 2nd Battalion, The Military Train – the transport division in the days when the horse was the main vehicle.

In late 1857, when the Indian Mutiny was at its height, Murphy's battalion was sent to Lucknow where around 1,000 British soldiers, led by Sir Henry Havelock from Sunderland, were besieged in dreadful conditions. The siege was successfully lifted, although Sir Henry himself perished and was buried under a mango tree.

Murphy's men then set off after the mutineers' leader, Koer Singh of Azimghur. In the ensuing battle, an officer fell from his saddle and lay wounded on the ground with sepoys all around. Murphy bravely rushed over and, with Private Samuel Morley, he fought back-to-back over the body of their fallen comrade, killing five sepoys, until help arrived.

Murphy was severely wounded five times and, along with Morley, was awarded the VC. At Windsor Castle on 4 January 1860 he was presented with the medal by Queen Victoria herself.

Over the next decade, Murphy rose to become a farrier major. He married an Irish girl, Mary, and they lived with their children in army accommodation at Aldershot. On 26 January 1872, he was caught allowing a civilian to leave the barracks with six bushels of oats and 12 pounds of hay. Explanations vary. Some say it was because the poor civilian couldn't afford to feed his horse; others think that Murphy was simply supplementing his meagre army wages, although the revenue from the theft of a sack of oats and a barrowful of hay would barely have bought a drink – hardly a hanging offence.

'For God's sake, look it over this time,' shouted Murphy at his court martial on 5 March 1872. 'It will ruin me.'

It was not looked over. Murphy was sentenced to nine months' hard labour. He was stripped of his rank, his £10 pa pension and his VC, and his wife and children were turned out of their accommodation. It did ruin him.

Once he'd served his sentence, he was discharged from the army as medically unfit, probably as a result of those five severe wounds. Barely able to work and without a pension he was condemned to a life of poverty. He wound up in the North East, trudging around pit communities looking for blacksmithing work.

His plight came to the attention of Sir Henry Havelock's son Sir Harry, who had inherited Blackwell Grange on the outskirts of Darlington in 1880. Sir Harry had been at Lucknow – he, like Murphy, had won a VC during the Indian Mutiny – and he took pity on the brave man whose one crime had wiped out twenty years of exemplary service.

In the late 1880s, he employed Murphy as a labourer on the Blackwell estate, and gave him an estate cottage. In 1889, when his wife was admitted into Winterton Asylum, near Sedgefield, he was living in one-bedroomed Wilton Lodge. Sir Harry also badgered the British government into restoring Murphy's pension.

When Murphy died of pneumonia aged sixty-three on 4 April 1893, he was an ironworker living at No. 22 Vulcan Street, Albert Hill, which was built on Allan family land (indeed, Lucknow Street is just a stone's throw away). Three of his sons had been killed fighting in foreign fields, and a fourth was away on active service, so Sir Harry followed his old comrade's coffin to the grave and paid for the headstone.

DID YOU KNOW?

Wilton Lodge was the gatehouse for Wilton House, which was built in 1867 for Miss Ann Allan, an eccentric relative of the Havelock-Allans of Blackwell Grange. She dressed in the fashions of a century earlier, and slept with a loaded blunderbuss in one hand and a rope, attached to a bell on the roof of the house, in the other. She died aged eighty-six in 1887 when her clothes caught fire. Wilton House is now a nursing home.

In 1920, George V rehabilitated Murphy's memory, saying that the VC could never be forfeited 'no matter the crime committed'. The king reasoned that the medal was awarded for outstanding split-second valour, not for a lifetime of good behaviour. That didn't stop his grave becoming overgrown, but in 1985, the headstone was repaired and in 2004, his regiment – by now called the Royal Logistics Corps – was stationed in a newly built camp near Basra in Iraq, which it called 'the Murphy Lines'.

The Fighting Bradfords

The Fighting Bradfords, Thomas, George, James and Roland, in the back garden of their home in Milbank Road.

Sir Thomas Bradford (1886–1966) DSO.

Above left: G. N. Bradford (1887–1918) VC.

Above middle: James Bradford (1889–1917) MC.

Above right: Roland Bradford (1892–1917) MC VC.

The entrance to the family home in Milbank Road.

Darlington Memorial Hospital was built in memory of the townsmen who died in the First World War, with the entrance dedicated to the Bradford brothers.

BRADFORD GEORGE NICHOLSON V.C.

BRADFORD ROLAND BOYS V.C. M.C.

BRADFORD JAMES BARKER M.C.

The three Bradford brothers' names on the wall inside the Memorial Hospital remembrance hall.

Author Chris Lloyd visits the grave of Brig-Gen Roland Bradford in Hermies Cemetery in northern France.

The four Bradford brothers – Thomas, George, James and Roland – and their sister, Amy, were all born in Witton Park, in south Durham, where their ferocious father, George, was a colliery manager. In 1894, when the youngest, Roland, was two, they moved to a farmhouse at Morton Palms, on the eastern edge of Darlington, apparently because their father felt it would be character forming for them to walk 4 miles into school and back every day in all weathers.

Four years later, they moved into Milbank Road in the west end of town. This large Victorian house, just around the corner from the Queen Elizabeth Grammar School, which they all attended, was the house they called home.

The eldest son, Thomas, was the only one of the four to survive the First World War, even though he joined the 8th Battalion of the Durham Light Infantry before it had begun. At the second Battle of Ypres in April 1915, his company was surrounded, but amid incredible carnage – of the 200 men he had left Newcastle station with at the beginning of the month, 180 were either dead, injured or missing by the end of the month – he showed such bravery that he was awarded the Distinguished Service Order.

He was then posted to Ireland to train young officers, rising to become a colonel. A great cricketer – he once scored 207 not out in ninety minutes in a Durham Senior League match – he later became chairman of the Durham County Conservative Association, stood twice for Parliament, and was knighted in 1939. In 1942 served as High Sheriff of County Durham and he lived to 1966, when he was eighty.

The first to die was the third brother, James, a second lieutenant with the 18th Durham Light Infantry. He was wounded on the Somme in August 1916, but after recovering in Milbank Road returned to the front where, near Hebuterne on 3 March 1917, he was awarded a Military Cross. His citation said that it was 'for conspicuous gallantry and devotion to duty. He gallantly led his men into the enemy's trench, capturing many prisoners and two machine guns. He himself killed three of the enemy. Later he succeeded in repelling a determined enemy counter attack.'

He was killed a month later at Arras, aged twenty-seven.

The next to die was the youngest, Roland. Serving with the Durham Light Infantry, he quickly won promotion to colonel during the trench warfare of 1915–16, until, on 1 October, he was leading the 9th DLI as it prepared to go into battle once more. Ninety minutes before the whistles blew, the commanding officer of the neighbouring 6th DLI was struck by shellfire, leaving Roland – himself carrying a long-standing wound for which he had refused treatment – to take command of both battalions.

In twenty-four hours of unrelenting, unremitting fighting, the Durhams made it through the heavy shelling into the first German trenches. They saw off an enemy counter-attack and dug themselves in. Finally, on 3 October, after nearly twenty days fighting on the frontline near Eaucourt L'Abbaye, what was left of the battalions was stood down.

It was only a brief respite because on 5 November, Roland led his men in a raid on the Butte de Warlencourt – a strange mound, 40 feet high, that stood out like a sore thumb in the flatlands around the Somme. After two days of fighting in the porridgey quagmire of the fields around the Butte, the DLI were beaten back, so on 25 November, the battalion was at rest when it heard that Roland was to receive the Victoria Cross for his actions at Eaucourt L'Abbaye. The men joyously chaired him around the camp, although he modestly said it was recognition for them all.

His citation said: 'By his fearless conduct under fire of all description and his skilful leadership of the two battalions, regardless of all danger, he succeeded in rallying the attack, and captured and defended the objective.'

It concluded that by his 'most conspicuous bravery and good leadership in attack, he saved the situation'. Aged twenty-four, he was the youngest recipient of the nation's highest award for bravery in the First World War.

Roland stayed on the Somme with his men until the following summer when, under pressure from senior officers, he reluctantly went to London to receive the medal from the king on 2 June. Then he dashed up to Darlington and, eschewing the pomp and ceremony proposed by the mayor, he paid a flying visit to his mother, and Annie, the newly widowed wife of his brother James. As he left his home in Milbank Road, he must have known there was a good chance that he wouldn't live long enough to see it again.

Back on the Western Front, he led 9th DLI so well that on 4 November, he was promoted to brigadier-general. At the age of twenty-five, he remains the youngest member of the British Army to hold this exalted rank.

It didn't last long. He led his men into the Battle of Cambrai, on the Somme, and then fell back for rest and recuperation. On the morning of 30 November, he was flukishly killed outright by shrapnel from a stray shell.

This left just one brother: George, who always referred to himself by his initials, G. N. He'd joined the Royal Navy in 1902, perhaps to escape his tyrannical father, but had spent much of the war frustrated by the navy's inactivity – especially as he heard of his brothers' derring-do.

His chance came in April 1918 when the British wanted to stop the German U-boats harassing shipping in the English Channel. The U-boats were disappearing into Zeebrugge harbour and down a 7-mile canal to Bruges where they were safely out of reach.

So a plan was hatched to block the canal by sinking blockships in Zeebrugge harbour. To manoeuvre the blockships into place, the Germans' defensive positions on top of the mole – the man-made harbour – would have to be taken out first, which meant landing vessels alongside the harbour wall and charging into the teeth of the guns.

It was to be such a dangerous mission that volunteers who were single men were sought. Step forward Lieutenant-Commander G. N. Bradford, who was put in charge of *Iris II*, one of the three advance ships attacking the guns.

On the evening of 22 April 1918, a mini-armada of seventy-five ships and 1,700 men set out. As the clock ticked past midnight, which meant that not only was it now St George's Day but also G. N.'s thirty-first birthday, they lit a smokescreen to hide their advance from watching eyes.

However, when they were a quarter-of-a-mile out, the wind abruptly changed direction and whipped away the screen, leaving the advance ships naked and vulnerable before the guns.

They raced into position at foot of the tall harbour wall, but the squall whipped up large waves. As the men on the decks placed their landing ladders against the wall, the surge of the swell snapped them like firewood.

G. N. could see the operation was doomed unless his ship could somehow be tied to the harbour so the men could get ashore. This was his moment...

Iris II had a derrick, or crane, fixed to its deck. With the ship pitching sickeningly, with the deck awash with bullets and blood, G. N. picked up a parapet anchor and climbed to the top of the crane.

There he waited for the right moment. The derrick swayed violently and the shells rained down, but he waited until a wave lifted the *Iris II* up so the top of the crane was practically level with the top of the harbour wall.

Then he jumped. He landed, as planned, on top of the wall and triumphantly secured his anchor. But in the same split second, as he must have known, the wave passed. *Iris II* dropped out of view, leaving him utterly alone, with every German gunner training their fire upon his silhouette.

The citation for his VC says:

> Immediately after hooking on the parapet anchor, Lt-Cmdr Bradford was riddled with bullets from machine guns and fell into the sea between the mole and the ship.
>
> Lt-Cmdr Bradford's action was one of absolute self-sacrifice; without a moment's hesitation, he went to certain death, recognising in such action lay the only possible chance of securing Iris II and enabling her storming parties to land.

Those parties took out the gun emplacements, allowing the three blockships to be guided into place and successfully scuttled. For the British, it was an enormous victory won by tub-thumping, chest-beating heroes like G. N. who restored the public's faith in their much-vaunted Royal Navy.

However, the British had lost 227 dead and 356 wounded, whereas the Germans had lost just eight dead and ten wounded, plus they were only mildly inconvenienced by having three bits of British scrap lying in the harbour.

Bradford's body was washed up on a beach 2 miles from Zeebrugge at Blankenberge a couple of days later. The Germans buried it with full military honours.

Nearly a year later, his mother, Amy, went to Buckingham Palace to collect his VC and every year thereafter until her own death in 1951, at the age of ninety-two, she pinned it alongside Roland's VC and her sons' other medals and proudly attended Remembrance Day services. They are the only brothers to win VCs in the First World War.

DID YOU KNOW?
At the start of the First World War, Darlington was one of the first fifty towns in the country to respond to the plea of Lord Kitchener, the Secretary of State for War, and form a 'Pals' battalion – groups of friends who signed up together and went off to war together. Among the earliest signatories in August 1914 was Alix Oliffe Liddle, a Pease and Partners clerk who lived with Clara, his wife of five months, in Sylvan Grove.

Andrew Mynarski

Andrew Mynarski, one of the very few to win a VC on the uncorroborated account of a single witness.

The statue of Mynarski outside what was the officers' mess at RAF Middleton St George – now Teesside Airport.

The aircrew sat on the grass beside their Lancaster bomber at RAF Middleton St George on 12 June 1944, idly whiling away the time before they embarked upon their thirteenth mission. One of them casually picked a four-leaf clover. He twirled the lucky emblem between his fingers like a tiny aeroplane propellor before handing it to his closest buddy.

'Here, Pat,' said Andrew Mynarski to George Patrick Brophy. 'You take it.'

Hours later, the Canadian crew were shot down over France. Brophy had 'a miraculous escape' and survived, and Mynarski went down in a blaze of bravery that won him a posthumous Victoria Cross.

They were in Lancaster KB726 VR-A, of the Royal Canadian Air Force, piloted by Canadian-born Flying Officer Art de Breyne, whose mother came from Durham City and whose grandfather was from Winston, near Darlington. On that night – 12 June into 13 June – they were one of 671 British aircraft sent to attack the German supply lines in France which were threatening to stop the Allied advances made in the week since D-Day. KB726 was tasked with hitting the important railway junction at Cambrai, but as it crossed the French coast, it was caught by a searchlight. De Breyne threw the bomber into a dive, desperately trying to escape the deadly glare.

As they descended to 2,000 feet, Brophy screamed through the intercom that there was a German fighter at six o'clock. De Breyne threw the Lancaster into a corkscrew, but it was too late. Three shots from the Junkers tore into it: two knocked out the port engines; the third ripped into the fuselage, and set fire to the hydraulic fuel, which operated the door to the rear gunner's glass dome.

De Breyne ordered his crew to bail out. Brophy immediately looked at his watch; he swore it said thirteen minutes after midnight on June 13 on the crew's thirteenth mission.

At 1,300 feet, Mynarski aborted his jump as he saw, through the burning fuselage, his best friend Brophy frantically trying to break out of the glass-domed rear turret. He crawled through the fire and, grabbing an axe, tried to smash his way through the shatterproof glass. The axe just bounced off. In desperation, he crazily dived at the dome with his bare hands.

'By now he was a mass of flames below the waist,' recalled Brophy in his article. 'Seeing him like that, I forgot everything else. Above the roar of the whine of our engine, I screamed: 'Go back, Andy! Get out!'.'

Realising the futility of the situation, Mynarski slunk back on his hands and knees, never taking his eyes from his condemned friend. He reached the escape hatch, pulled himself up to his full height and in his flaming clothes came to attention, saluted the stricken Brophy, and jumped.

Brophy curled into the crash-landing position knowing it was pointless as just beneath him was 5 tons of high explosives. 'Everything came at once,' wrote Brophy, 'the ground's dark blur, the slam of a thousand sledgehammers, the screech of ripping metal.'

Remarkably, as the Lancaster slid along the ground, a tree ripped off a wing, which threw it into a demented spin that, miraculously, released the mechanism in the rear turret and tossed Brophy clear. As he hit the ground, he blacked out, only to be brought round by an earth-juddering explosion when the broken bomber exploded.

Brophy had escaped without a scratch, although when he pulled off his helmet, most of his hair came off with it. For eleven weeks, the French Resistance was passed from safe house to safe house until he made it back to England, where he learned the fate of his colleagues. Two had been taken prisoner and three had been rescued. One – Andy Mynarski – was seen falling from the sky with his parachute in flames. He'd crashed into a field, his clothes still alight on impact, and had died after an hour so of severe burns.

He is buried in a war cemetery near Amiens. Two years after his death, the twenty-seven-year-old was posthumously awarded the Victoria Cross, becoming the first Canadian airman to receive the award, and one of very few to win it on the uncorroborated account of a single witness.

In 2005, *The Northern Echo* was part of a campaign that successfully erected a statue of Mynarski in full flying gear looking to the skies and saluting – just as he saluted his friend Brophy in those final moments in the burning plane over France.

William McMullen

A fateful fourteen minutes turned William McMullen into a hero. At 8.35 p.m. on 13 January 1945, he was over Middlesbrough at the controls of his Lancaster bomber, returning to his RAF Middleton St George after a routine training flight; by 8.49 p.m., he was dead in a field, surrounded by burning wreckage, on the eastern outskirts of Darlington and was being proclaimed a hero for saving the town from a calamitous impact.

McMullen had probably been born in Toronto in 1912 – 'probably' because when he died in distant Darlington, his age was variously reported as being twenty-nine or thirty-three. Ever since he had been young, McMullen had loved flying, and although he worked as a sales representative for Coca Cola, he spent his spare money on flying lessons.

Pilot Officer William Stuart McMullen, who didn't qualify for a gallantry medal as he saved Darlington while on a training flight.

Above and left: The McMullen memorial on McMullen Road.

At the start of the war, he was pushing thirty. As only younger men were considered as pilots, he manipulated his age, although airmen gave him the nickname 'Grandad'.

McMullen won his wings in November 1942 and in 1944 left his wife, Thelma, and daughter, Donna, five, and came to England. Meanwhile, on August 16, six Canadian fliers became available when their pilot broke his leg after they all baled out of their burning Lancaster over France. They teamed up with McMullen and on Christmas Eve were posted to RAF Middleton St George.

On Saturday 13 January, as they hadn't been on a mission for three weeks, they were sent on a three-hour cross-country navigation exercise to keep them sharp.

They set out at 5.47 p.m., just as the daylight was fading, aboard Lancaster KB793. It was all routine radar stuff carried out at 10,000 feet over the North York Moors. At 8.35 p.m., McMullen called the airfield for 'joining instructions', and instructed his engineer, Sgt 'Lew' Lewellin, to keep the engines at 1,950 rpm so the descent speed would be 200 mph. Lewellin wrote in his log: 'All temperatures and pressures normal. All four engines running evenly.'

However, there was a fault in the outer port Rolls-Royce Merlin engine. Flight Sgt Steve Ratsoy, the wireless operator, reported that it was emitting a shower of sparks and was glowing red. McMullen ordered Lewellin to shut it down.

As he did so, Ratsoy reported that a sheet of flame shot from the engine, that the red glow was spreading along the wing and that there now appeared to be flames licking at the engine cover.

It later transpired that the feathering pipe was not protected against fire and had already burned away. Therefore, when Lewellin pressed the button to shut the engine down, he was actually forcing oil out of the pipe so that it fell onto the red-hot surfaces, causing the sheet of flame. Rather than stopping the fire, he was pouring oil onto it...

At 2,500 feet over Acklam, with three engines still working and McMullen still in control of the plane, he gave the order to abandon the aircraft. Jump, jump, jump...

DID YOU KNOW?
RAF Middleton St George was the most northerly of all Bomber Command airfields. Work creating it began in 1939, and it opened in January 1941. Locals and aircrew nicknamed it RAF Goosepool after a nearby farm; aircrew used that name so often that German intelligence became convinced there must be a second airfield, as well as RAF Middleton St George, that they had yet to locate somewhere in Durham.

The first five parachuted perfectly downwards and landed neatly in a line along what became the A66 between Elton and Sadberge. At 600 feet, engineer Lewellin was last to leave. As he stood by the main door, he looked over to McMullen at the controls and gesticulated that he should get ready to jump next, but with hundreds of houses in the east end of Darlington – the town's population then was 80,000 – fast approaching, McMullen is said to have shouted back: 'No, it's only me for it. There are thousands down below.'

McMullen could have made it to safety – Lewellin landed unscathed 500 yards from the crash site – but in that split second, he chose to remain.

Hundreds of Darlingtonians, drawn by the unusual sound of an engine in trouble, came rushing from their homes. They saw KB793 flying in broad circles above the Eastbourne district. It was still at 600 feet, but the port wing was by now well ablaze.

Suddenly, the Lancaster ceased its circles and dived steeply. Its undercarriage skimmed the rooftops of the streets named after waterfowl, and having cleared the last of them in Lingfield Lane, plunged to earth. It cartwheeled 150 yards across the field of Lingfield Farm, losing various bits of flaming fuselage as it went, its fuel tanks exploding vividly and its bullets dancing across the ridges like firecrackers until they struck the hay and oats in the farm's Dutch barn, which immediately blazed brightly.

The pilot was dead, killed on impact. He'd been catapulted, still strapped to his seat, 120 yards out of the windscreen, but his flying boots were found later in the aircraft, still attached to the rubber pedals in the cockpit where he had remained in those dying seconds.

All Darlington was convinced McMullen hadn't jumped because he wanted to save them. They christened him the 'Gallant Airman' and hailed him a hero. He had stayed with his stricken aircraft, battling to keep it away from their homes, when he could have jumped and saved his own life, but because this was a training flight, he was not eligible for any award.

The official accident report said that a mechanical fault in a piston had caused the initial fire, and it concluded: 'It is also noted that the pilot retained control of the aircraft sufficiently long enough to avoid crashing into the built-up area of Darlington.'

The town's mayor, Jimmy Blumer, said: 'By his actions, the pilot realised that he was steering himself to certain death. Not only Darlington, but the whole of the district was stirred to profound admiration and gratitude which could not be expressed in words at this act of supreme sacrifice.'

McMullen was buried in Stonefall Cemetery, in Harrogate, and the town collected £1,000, which it offered it to his widow and young daughter back in Canada. Thelma refused it, saying it would be best put to use in war-ravaged Britain. Lingfield Lane near the crash site was renamed McMullen Road, and the money was used to endow two children's cots at the Memorial Hospital.

Mayor Blumer wrote to Thelma to say: 'For sheer self-sacrificing heroism, your husband's action will be remembered and honoured by the people of Darlington for years to come.'

DID YOU KNOW?
The Royal Canadian Air Force arrived at RAF Middleton St George in October 1942 and remained until flying its last raid on 2 June 1945. Since the airfield became operational in 1941, it had lost 279 bombers and 1,255 aircrew. A further 325 groundcrew had also died, taking total casualties to 1,580.

7. Remarkable Women

Elizabeth Pease Nichol

Elizabeth Pease as a young lady in Darlington. (Picture courtesy of the Darlington Centre for Local Studies)

Elizabeth Pease was born in 1807 in Feethams, the grandest mansion in Darlington, which stood where the Town Hall is today. She was a cousin of the railway Peases, and she was fired unfairly. She believed that all men were equal, and so campaigned vigorously against slavery.

In June 1840, she attended the World Anti-Slavery Convention in London and was horrified to discover that women were not only forbidden from speaking but also had to be fenced off behind a bar and curtains. This inequality fired her further, and she became a 'moral force Chartist'. The Chartists were working class agitators demanding political

The Mechanics' Institute in Skinnergate. Elizabeth Pease was the greatest benefactor to this place of learning, and laid the foundation stone in 1853 with a fish slice.

reform. The ruling elite of Elizabeth's day regarded them as revolutionaries – even though today, all but one of their six campaigning points are crucial to our constitution – but Elizabeth invited them to Feethams because they supported 'the equality of women's rights'.

In 1853, because she also believed in equality of educational opportunities, she gave the largest donation – £400 (around £50,000 in today's values) – for the building of the £2,300 Mechanics' Institute in Skinnergate, and she was asked to lay the foundation stone on 12 May 1853, using a 'silver trowel which was judiciously contrived to serve as a fish slice'.

Three weeks later, Elizabeth, forty-six, married Dr John Pringle Nichol in an independent chapel off Northgate. Dr Nichol was the professor of astronomy at Glasgow University and was considered to be the greatest astronomer of his day with an ability to fire the interest of the ordinary person in the heavens – he was the Brian Cox of his day. But things did not get better for Elizabeth because Dr Nichol was a Presbyterian, and it was forbidden for a Quaker to marry outside her faith. Edward 'Father of the Railways' Pease wrote that this was 'a union very much advised against and disapproved by all her friends'.

So, because of love, Elizabeth was 'disowned' by the Darlington Quakers and lived out the rest of her days in Scotland. In fact, her last visit to her hometown seems to have been on 1 September 1854, when she returned with Dr Nichol to perform the official opening of the Mechanics Institute.

Dr Nichol lived just five years after their marriage – 'Alas! Alas! Widow and desolate,' she wrote in her diary – and in widowhood she threw herself into numerous causes in her new home city of Edinburgh: peace, temperance, anti-vivisection and especially women's suffrage. She died in Edinburgh in 1890, and in 2013, the Auld Reekie considered erecting a statue in honour of the Darlington lady who had done so much for equality.

Darlington, of course, already has such a memorial to her beliefs: the grand Mechanics Institute, although since the closure of its restaurant and nightclub in 2019, it is now looking for a new future.

Mary Jane Allen

Mary Jane Allen's remarkable memorial in West Cemetery. The horse has lost all of its legs, although you can still tell that it is a stallion.

Mary Jane Allen's Excelsior big top on the Green Tree Fields behind Skinnergate.

The Excelsior Circus came to Darlington in late 1873 and pitched its big top on the Green Tree Fields behind the Friends Meeting House in Skinnergate.

The proprietor was Frederick Allen and the star of the show was his wife, Mary Jane Allen, whose bareback horse riding was the most eagerly anticipated item on the bill. Her love of horses came from her father, John Brown, of Morpeth, Northumberland, who was one of the last post boys to deliver the mail on horseback. In turn, she passed her love onto her four sons, who starred with her in the family's Christmas pantomime, 'Harlequin Tom Tally Ho! or Ride-a-Cock-horse to Banbury Cross'.

While in Darlington, Mary Jane contracted bronchitis, and died on 19 February 1874, after four days' illness. She was only thirty-two. For one day, Mr Allen closed his circus so he could bury his wife in West Cemetery beneath a flamboyant stone memorial, which features a galloping horse.

Time has not been kind to the memorial because the horse, which is still clearly a stallion, has lost its legs so that it looks as if it is flying. Until at least 1956 relatives of Mary Jane were still leaving flowers beneath it on the anniversary of her untimely death.

Clara Curtis Lucas

For decades, Clara Curtis Lucas led a peaceful, yet forceful, campaign for women to get the vote, and she secured her place in Darlington history by becoming the first woman in the town to be elected to a public office.

She was born in Thirsk in 1853, the daughter of a railwayman, and was educated at Polam Hall School, which, in those days, was a radically minded hotbed of female equality. After leaving school, she ran night classes in a bid to spread educational opportunity, and as chairman of the Darlington Women's Suffrage Society, she toured the region, speaking at meetings.

Clara Curtis Lucas, Darlington's first female councillor. (Picture courtesy of Darlington Centre for Local Studies)

Clara Curtis Lucas built Fieldhead, in Abbey Road.

How *The Northern Echo* reported Clara's groundbreaking success in the polls.

In 1894, she was voted onto the Education Board, which ran the town's schools, but she could go no further until August 1907 when the Qualification of Women Act was passed enabling women ratepayers to stand for the council. Miss Lucas put herself forward in 1915 as Darlington's first ever female candidate. She stood in the Cockerton ward, where she came third with 483 votes, 105 votes behind the poll-topping man, but twenty-five ahead of the chap in fourth so enough to win a seat.

DID YOU KNOW?
Ann Allan was the third generation of her family to live in Blackwell Grange, which she inherited in 1753. She was known as 'The Good Miss Allan' because there was always a bowl of pennies in the Grange porch for passers-by in need, and she employed a 'feline fisherman' at Hurworth to catch fish fresh from the Tees to feed her large population of cats, which roamed wild throughout Blackwell. Her funeral, at St Cuthbert's Church, was attended by around 10,000 people (Darlington's population was only around 3,500). This attendance may have been because so many people had been touched by her charity, or because a dole of a shilling for adults and sixpence for children was handed out.

The mayor, Councillor J. G. Harbottle, 'specially congratulated her as being one of the few women in England who was privileged to sit at the council table'. She responded with a 'well received' victory speech, thanking those who had voted for her and saying 'she hoped they would never have cause to regret sending a woman to the Darlington County Council.'

However, such was the windbaggery of the twenty-seven male councillors and aldermen at her first, lengthy council meeting that she said at the end: 'If we're going to be here all this time every month, I'll bring my knitting.'

Following the February 1918 Representation of the Peoples Act, which gave the first women the vote, Miss Lucas must have taken her place in the polling booth in the December 1918 general election, and she chaired the next meeting of the Suffrage Society, saying that the new goal was to get equal pay for female and male teachers.

Then she fell ill and was confined to the newly built house – Fieldhead in Abbey Road – which she shared with her spinster sister, Alice, where she died on 14 April 1919, aged sixty-five.

'A woman of strong personality, holding advanced and independent views, she was essentially a pioneer, and in her advocacy of the woman's cause had to meet with a considerable amount of opposition which, however, only strengthened her determination to win for her sex equal rights with those of men,' said *The Northern Echo* in its obituary.

Katherine Pease Routledge

Katherine Pease as a young girl in Darlington. (Picture courtesy of Darlington Centre for Local Studies)

Katherine Routledge had to escape Darlington. She had to get away from the voices in her head, the demons in her family tree, and the town centre, which is looked down upon by an oversize statue of her domineering grandfather, Joseph Pease.

She ended up 8,420 miles away in perhaps the remotest place on Earth: Easter Island in the Pacific Ocean, which is 1,350 miles from its nearest neighbour, Pitcairn Island. There she stood dwarfed beneath the island's enormous, enigmatic stone figures – the mysterious monuments to another culture's ancestor worship.

Katherine was born in 1864 in Greencroft West, a mansion that was built for her father, Gurney Pease, by his father, Joseph. It was in Coniscliffe Road, one of eleven neighbouring Pease estates, and in the shadow of Joseph's opulent Southend mansion, which is now Duncan Bannatyne's Grange Hotel.

Joseph Pease, Katherine's grandfather, is Darlington's greatest son and features on the only statue in town.

Katherine's grandfather, Joseph Pease, looks down on Darlington in much the same way as the heads of Easter Island look down on successive generations there.

Southend, Katherine's childhood home, which she had to escape.

The plaque commemorating Katherine on her former home, which is now a hotel.

In her 2003 book about Katherine, *Among Stone Giants*, Dr Jo Anne Van Tilburg, of the University of California, tells how Joseph cast a domineering pall over his family of twelve children. In Katherine's childhood, two maiden aunts, Jane and Emma, loomed large. They never escaped from Southend, even though Jane, when seventeen, had fallen in love with a young man when staying at Joseph's seaside retreat of Cliffe House, in Marske. The young man had been an Anglican and, even though he rose to become the suitably sober and sensible Archdeacon of Cleveland, Joseph forbade his daughter from marrying outside their Quaker sect. So Jane died a spinster in 1894, the last mourner to leave her graveside after her burial at the Skinnergate Friends Meeting House being a grey-haired Anglican clergyman.

The death of Joseph on 8 February 1872 sent Gurney into terminal depression, and he died four months later, aged only thirty-three, leaving an estate worth £17 million today. His wife, Kate, who was increasingly bedridden, was moved into Woodside, a large mansion off Blackwell Lane (now demolished), where Katherine was effectively brought up by her nanny, Mrs Hopper, and the butler, 'Bossy' Bosomworth.

Her eldest brother, Harold, probably suffered from schizophrenia, and was locked away, Bronte-esque, screaming. After attacking his wife in a London hotel, he was returned to a sanatorium for the rest of his days.

Katherine, too, inherited her share of mental unease, but she also suffered from the acute tedium of being a wealthy Pease girl waiting for marriage. She hung around in Darlington until she was twenty-five before forcing her way out of the family cocoon and into Oxford University, where her history studies were interrupted by ill health.

Back in Darlington, she hankered after a way out and in 1902, she sailed for South Africa with a female university friend to do field study on the end of the Boer War. Out there, she met an Australian explorer-archaeologist, William Scoresby Routledge. They married on 6 August 1906, in the Skinnergate Meeting House, the silence of their Quaker service shattered by a tremendous thunderstorm. 'Life can't be all happiness,' said Katherine, and her marriage bed was certainly not made of the traditional roses.

Scoresby had negotiated a £20,000 pay-off from the Peases and had gained a wealthy wife who could fund his travels. For her side of the bargain, Katherine had found her escape route. Whether they were ever lovers is questionable, and they lived separately on most of their expeditions.

They spent two years exploring the tribal customs of east Africa, many of which had never been witnessed before by a white woman. Then to Easter Island, an extraordinary voyage of discovery, where they arrived on 28 March 1914. Katherine lived under canvas or in a makeshift ranch and became the first archaeologist to record the statues and the folklore of their people. It was the happiest time of her life, and it was groundbreaking. When she returned to England, she was greeted with astonishment and by George V, who wanted news of his smallest colony.

After publication of books and papers, she and Scoresby went on a second major voyage among the peoples of the Polynesian islands scattered across the Pacific Ocean. She made some valuable discoveries but could not repeat the success of Easter Island.

News from home reached her, first of the death of her mother and then of her favourite brother, Wilson, who had anchored her in reality.

She bought an extravagant house in Hyde Park Gardens, London, and paid Scoresby to stay with her. Surrounded by mementoes, she sunk into a reclusiveness inhabited by voices from her past, most prominently her grandfather, Joseph, and her great-grandfather, Edward, 'the Father of the Railways', whom she summoned up during seances. It was said that she had fallen under the spell of Angata, a witch doctor on Easter Island, and her younger brother, John Henry, said: 'This spook business seems to be practically sending her off her head.'

In 1928, her family took legal action to protect her (and her huge fortune) from herself. She locked Scoresby out of their house and, in Dr Tilburg's words, 'rose to a magnificent level of indignation'. She called the press to show them how she was camping in her own bathroom.

In February 1929, with the knowledge of her family and husband, she was dragged, kicking and screaming, out of her house into an ambulance disguised as a motor car and carried to Ticehurst, a lunatic asylum in Sussex.

'There, the great voyage that was her life ended on 13 December 1935, when Katherine Maria Pease Routledge, explorer, author, and brilliant brave-hearted woman, died of a cerebral thrombosis,' concluded Dr Tilburg.

Katherine had contributed enormously to the understanding of a long-lost faraway culture, but she had never been able to escape her own past in Darlington.

Emilie Hawkes Peacocke

In late Victorian times, women couldn't be journalists: they could not write, they could not do grammar and they certainly could not understand the complexities of the big issues of the day upon which they would be reporting.

Emilie Hawkes Marshall, though, went from Larchfield Street, where she was born in March 1882, to Fleet Street, where she became the *Daily Mail*'s first female reporter and then the *Daily Telegraph*'s first women's editor.

Larchfield Street, looking east towards Duke Street, in 1980. Emilie was born on 26 March 1882, in No. 2 – the white door on the right.

Larchfield Street today. Emilie's birthplace has been replaced by Buckden Court.

John Marshall, editor of *The Northern Echo*,
who taught Emilie all he knew.

Emilie was born to be a pioneering journalist. Her mother, Mildred Hawkes, was the
daughter of the editor of the *Newcastle Chronicle*, and her father, John Marshall, edited
The Northern Echo from 1883 until 1902.

They educated her at home – after a few years in Larchfield Street, they moved to No. 17,
Langholm Crescent, and then in the 1890s to No. 6, Victoria Road, which is now beneath
the flats beside Sainsbury's petrol station – and she avidly read her father's review copies
of the controversially fashionable 'new women' novels (the chicklit of the day).

Aged fifteen, Emilie studied shorthand and became a proofreader in her father's
Priestgate office, and aged sixteen, she followed a training plan devised by him to become
the *Echo*'s first female reporter and the only 'girl reporter' in the North East.

Once the paper had been put to bed at night, she would cycle home through the deserted
streets of Darlington with a thrill in her heart. 'I was filled with pride in the thought that
I was already in possession of the news of the day that the people still asleep in the dark,
silent houses would not learn till breakfast time,' she said.

Her father's time in the *Echo* editor's chair ended in 1902, when she was twenty. The
Echo was in financial difficulties with falling circulation due to Mr Marshall's strong
stance against the Boer War – principled but unpopular. He moved the family to London,
where he died in 1905, aged foty-nine.

Emilie struggled to find journalistic work as a woman. As a reporter on the *Church
Family Newspaper*, at one ecclesiastical meeting, a man spotted she was female and forced
her to sit behind a red silken cord, which meant she was officially non-existent.

Another former *Echo* editor, W. T. Stead, gave her a job on his new *Daily Paper*, but it closed after five weeks. She then became the first full-time female reporter on the *Daily Express*, although at first she was not allowed to use the staff room. She moved to *The Tribune*, a newly established Liberal paper, and became friendly with the suffragettes. At the suggestion of Labour leader Keir Hardie, Emilie was in the House of Commons when he introduced a women's suffrage resolution. She was the only journalist present as MPs filibustered his motion out of time, causing the suffragettes in the gallery to explode in a leaflet-throwing rage – a great scoop.

As the suffragette movement grew more violent, Prime Minister H. H. Asquith blocked Downing Street to keep the women protestors from his door. The *Daily Mail* employed Emilie as its first female reporter to cover the story, and she spotted a loophole in Royal Mail regulations that allowed women to be posted. At her instigation, the suffragettes mailed themselves to No. 10 Downing Street, thus breaching the security, reaching the prime minister and gaining Emilie another great exclusive.

However, Emilie had a secret of her own: she had married Herbert Peacocke, a journalist on the *Mail*'s great rival, the *Express*. When her *Mail* bosses discovered this, they sacked her – she was sleeping with the enemy and, worst of all, liable to fall pregnant at any moment.

During the First World War, Emilie had a daughter, Marguerite, and worked for the Ministry of Information 'writing articles celebrating the courage and resourcefulness of women', according to her entry in the Dictionary of National Biography.

Her husband, Herbert, fought in the trenches of the Western Front and was gassed at Ypres. He returned a shell of a man, dying in 1931, and Emilie had to work to support their family. The *Express* took her on, and she covered Nancy Astor's successful campaign in 1919 to become the first female MP to take her seat in the Commons.

Emilie moved to edit the *Express*' women's page. She had long railed against the inherent discrimination of a women's page, but under her, the articles became broad enough to appeal to men as well. In 1928, the *Daily Telegraph* poached her to edit its new women's section, and she stayed there until her retirement in 1940.

She died in Kensington in 1964, a radical pioneer who pushed at the barriers that held women back and championed their causes.

DID YOU KNOW?
Miss Fanny Smallbones became the second principal of the Darlington Training College for Mistresses (later the Arts Centre) in Vane Terrace in 1877. Two years later, she caused great consternation among the college committee when she announced that she intended to marry her vice-principal, William Spafford. The committee felt, after much agonising, that no husband could take orders from his wife, and so sacked them both and asked them to reapply for their jobs. After the selection procedure, Mr Spafford was promoted to principal and poor Fanny, because she was a woman, was demoted to be lady superintendent – a position she held until she retired in 1913.

Mary Lawson

Mary Lawson, the Scala Pet.

Mary Lawson – she was the Posh to Fred Perry's Becks.

Mary Lawson was the railwayman's daughter who became engaged to the greatest sporting star of her generation. She was born in a humble terraced street and died in the arms of her fabulously wealthy husband beneath a German air raid. She was the child star with a little kiss curl. She first wowed audiences in the Scala cinema in Darlington, but went on to win hearts in Her Majesty's Theatre in Sydney, Australia.

One stage magazine described her as a 'petite, retrousee-nosed, earnest North of England girl'; others described her as Darlington's Gracie Fields.

She was born on 20 August 1910 at No. 58 Pease Street, off Yarm Road, the third of three children. Her father, Tommy, was a North Eastern Railway crane driver; her mother died when she was three and her elder sister, Dora, chaperoned her around the world.

Mary's career began when she was five, singing to injured servicemen who were billeted in the Feethams mansion in the Leadyard. She got a regular booking at the Scala cinema – now a bingo hall off Eldon Street – where she sang and danced while the projectionist changed the film reels. They called her 'the Scala Pet', or 'Little Mary Lawson' – a nickname she never grew out of as she didn't make it to five feet tall.

At twelve, the Dodmire schoolgirl made her professional debut in a musical comedy called *Sunshine Sally*, which opened at the Theatre Royal in Northgate. Its star was

MARY LAWSON, the clever little English comedienne, who is appearing in "Hold Everything" at the Theatre Royal.

Mary on the front cover of an Australian magazine, showing her trademark kiss curl.

Miss Dot Stephens, a well-known actress who was making her comeback, having lost a foot and all her toes in a railway accident. Called 'the pluckiest girl on the stage', Miss Stephens amazed the audience by dancing and cycling on her wooden appendages. But Little Mary Lawson stole the show with her rendition of 'Golden Curls'.

Sunshine Sally then toured the UK, ending Mary's full-time education. At the Lyceum Theatre in London in 1925, Mary – billed as 'a diminutive dancer' – was paired with an up-and-coming Max Wall, who was two years her senior. She went into provincial panto, which led to her being selected for the summer season at Frinton-on-Sea, Essex, in *The Lido Follies*. It doesn't sound glamorous, but the show was put together by Archie Pitt – married to Gracie Fields – who doubled Mary's wages to £4 a week.

The blue terraced house in Pease Street is where Mary grew up and where, at the height of her fame, she held a press conference.

That summer – 1928 – the *Daily Mail* launched its Search for a Seaside Stage Star. Gracie sent a telegram to the *Mail*'s theatrical correspondent William Pollock advising him to have a look at Mary. He labelled her 'the most promising girl I have seen' – it was as if Simon Cowell had announced that Mary had won X Factor. Within weeks, she was snapped up by a London impresario who catapulted her into the West End as last-minute replacement in the musical *Good News* at the Carlton Theatre. 'She was so successful that at the end, the whole of the cast, principals and chorus, crowded round and cheered the 17-year-old girl who had won her spurs,' said the *Daily Express*.

Good News toured the provinces, including two weeks at Newcastle Empire Theatre. The papers wrote it up as a homecoming, and in a brilliant piece of PR, every journalist called on Mary's humble home in Pease Street where they all found her doing the cleaning.

'In her handbag was a contract guaranteeing her an income of nearly £3,000-a year, but a visitor might have mistaken her for any of the 50 shilling-a-week typists and shop girls living in the same street,' wrote one. 'Attired in a plain skirt and a thoroughly sensible jumper – with sleeves rolled up for the fray – she dashed about energetically and washed and scrubbed and dusted.'

The lucrative contract sailed Mary and Dora off to Australia, via New York, for a year, and into filmland. In May 1934, tennis star Fred Perry visited her on the set of *Falling in Love*. They fell in love and became engaged.

It was a sensation. It was Posh and Becks for the pre-war generation, but the engagement only lasted eight months. Said Mary: 'Publicity has killed our romance. I am sick and tired of the ridiculous rumours and of being rung up time after time about some story or other.'

There was talk of reconciliation, but it never happened. Mary went on to make her most famous film, *Scrooge*, in 1935, and Fred went on to famously win Wimbledon in 1936. Mary appeared in fourteen films with stars such as Stanley Holloway, Vivien Leigh and Bud Flanagan, but only had eyes for the producer of *The Toilers of the Sea*, Francis W. L. C. Beaumont. The dramatic film, in which a steamer crashes onto Channel Islands rocks and the hero grapples with an 8-foot octopus, was shot in Sark where Beaumont's mother, Dame Sibyl, was the Seigneur – the feudal ruler. In November 1937, he asked for a divorce from his wife on the grounds of his adultery with Miss Mary Lawson, and the following year they married. Only Mary's father and sister witnessed the ceremony as Dame Sibyl was far from happy.

Tragically, it didn't last long. On 4 May 1941, the couple were with friends in Liverpool. For the eighth consecutive night, the city was struck by an air raid. As the sirens wailed, Dora and their friends retreated to the shelter while Mary and Francis – on a week's leave from the RAF – stayed in their room. The house was struck by a bomb and while those in the shelter survived, the couple in bed were killed. Mary was only thirty-one.

8. Amazing Men

Robert Stainsby

Able Seaman Robert Stainsby has an incredible – indeed, indelible – claim to fame. He was born in 1741, the third child of William and Hanna Stainsby, of Darlington. On 26 August 1768, he was one of ninety-four people aboard HM *Bark Endeavour* as Captain James Cook set sail from Plymouth to the southern hemisphere. On 13 April 1769, they'd reached Tahiti where Captain Cook in his journal noted how the natives 'paint their bodys Tattow as it is called in their language, this is done by inlaying the Colour of black under their skins in such a manner as to be indelible'.

The tattoo was made by pricking a black oil, from the candlenut, into the skin using sharp pieces of bone or shell. Cook said: 'This is a painful operation especially the tattowing their buttocks.'

A small party of British sailors plucked up courage to give it a go. Sydney Parkinson, a Scottish botanical illustrator, wrote in his diary on 13 July 1769: 'Mr Stainsby, myself, and some others of our company, underwent the operation, and had our arms marked.'

Tattooing had been around for millennia, but it is Cook's voyage that introduced the word to the English language – it is Polynesian for 'to mark' – and started the custom for sailors to get themselves inked. A Darlington lad seems to have been the very first to start this practice – if it wasn't Robert Stainsby, Premiership footballers might have nothing on their arms.

E. T. Pease

When an enormous cask brimming with 1,000 gallons of brandy arrived on a ship at a wharf in Stockton, it was so heavy that it broke the arm of the crane unloading it. The railway company, which was supposed to be transporting it to Darlington, took one look and refused to allow the vast vat onto its wagons until the contents had been decanted into smaller, lighter tuns.

Finally, when the cask – believed to be the largest ever imported into this country – reached its destination in Darlington, it was too large to get into the cellars beneath the Covered Market, and so coopers had to take it to pieces and reassemble it inside.

The man responsible for this barrel of gaffes was Edward Thomas Pease. His father, Thomas, was a cousin of the famous Edward 'Father of the Railways' Pease. They were Quakers until, in 1808, Thomas announced that he was stopping being a chemist on High Row and was becoming a wine merchant. It is said that this was such a shock to the temperance side of the family that Thomas was booted out of the teetotal Quakers and became an Anglican.

E. T. was the second generation to run the business, and in 1864, when the Covered Market was completed, he hired the cool cellars, which were perfect for storing his spirits.

The 1,000-gallon barrel of brandy photographed beneath Darlington's Covered Market.

In 1970s, when the market was restored, hundreds of full bottles of Pease wine were found laid on their sides amid the foundations of the town clock.

E. T. was a man of many interests. He was a JP, a freemason, an active member of the Darlington Charity Organisation Society, and also a leading member of the Pteridological Society of Great Britain – pteridologists are fern collectors and pteridomania was a mid-Victorian craze. In E. T.'s home of Oak Lea, in Woodlands Road (now beneath the hospital), he had 'a very fine collection of British ferns'.

He was a linguist and a traveller. In 1870, during the Franco-Prussian War, he was in Charente in the Cognac region of France, where the brandy distillers were worried about the Prussian army sweeping through and destroying their produce. He struck a deal, and, evading a Prussian blockade, successfully exported two huge casks: one containing 558 gallons of pale brandy, the other containing 315 gallons of light brandy.

Prussia won the war, and France was forced to pay reparations, much of which was to be raised by a tax on the wine producers. In 1875, to help the producers evade the tax, E. T. bought 1,000 gallons of pale brandy – worth more than £100,000 in today's values – which he imported in the record-breaking cask.

'The large derrick ordinarily used in relieving vessels of their most bulky cargo at Stockton wharf, gave way with a crash under the excessive strain of taking the cask off the steamer,' says a contemporary report. Heavy duty lifting gear was brought in, but still the railway company insisted half of the brandy should be siphoned off into seven

The barrel was too large to be taken through the door into the market cellars, so the brandy had to be decanted while it was taken to pieces and reassembled inside.

E. T. Pease lived in Woodland Road and was a generous benefactor of Holy Trinity Church (behind the tram).

smaller puncheons before the cask could be loaded onto the trucks. Such was its enormity that it filled two trucks, and when it reached Darlington, it couldn't fit into the cellars beneath the market.

'The cask had, therefore, to be entirely denuded of its remaining contents and taken to pieces by a competent staff of coopers,' says the report.

The town was filled with people celebrating the fiftieth anniversary of the opening of the Stockton & Darlington Railway. 'The enormous crowd who witnessed the arrival of the vat was doubtless as much impressed with its appearance as by any of the numerous sights in connection with the celebration of the railway jubilee,' says the report.

DID YOU KNOW?
Joseph Pease's 9-foot bronze statue on High Row – the only character statue in Darlington – is by Scottish sculptor George Anderson Lawson, who has statues in Liverpool, Ayr, Glasgow and Leicester, as well as in Chile, New Zealand and Australia. It was unveiled at 5 p.m. on 27 September 1875, which was the fiftieth anniversary of the opening of the Stockton & Darlington Railway, before a crowd of 100,000. In 1884, Lawson created a statue of John Vaughan, Joseph's friend and one of the founders of Middlesbrough. Around the bottom of each plinth are four friezes summing up the life of the industrialist above – the Darlington and Middlesbrough statues share a common frieze showing industry.

E. T. died at his home in Woodland Road in 1897, leaving an £85,000 fortune – around £10 million in today's values. In his will, he left £40 to his head cellarman, £10 to his second cellarman, and he 'desired that his horse Jumbo should not be sold but should be put out at grass or shot, as the executors may think best, and he commended to their careful attention his dog Bruin'. He left £4,000 to the parish of Holy Trinity, which was spent on extending the chancel and on building St Mary's Church in Cockerton.

His son, Frank, became the third generation to run the company, and in 1899 he had well-known local architect J. P. Prichett design a distinctive headquarters on Bakehouse Hill opposite the market. In 1939, when war broke out, all of the company's stock was transferred to the bakehouse cellars from the market cellars so that they could be used as air-raid shelters. It was at this point that the giant, record-breaking barrels were destroyed because they were taking up too much space. The business itself lasted until 1995 when Robin, the fifth generation, retired.

Frank Charles Bostock

The one thing, perhaps the only thing, that everyone knows about lion taming is that the fiercest king of the jungle is miraculously quelled by having the four legs of an upturned chair pointed at it. The man who discovered this amazing fact, and went on to make a globally renowned name for himself out of it, was born in Darlington.

EDMOND'S (LATE WOMBWELL'S,)

WINDSOR CASTLE and CRYSTAL PALACE MENAGERIE is this day (SATURDAY) and MONDAY in DARLINGTON.

Will visit RICHMOND on TUESDAY.
" LEYBURNE on WEDNESDAY,
" BEDALE on THURSDAY.

DELIMONICO, the Arabian Lion Chief, will exhibit his Prussian NEEDLE GUN, and drive the only pair of domesticated ZEBRAS in the world round the collection, prior to each performance with his 20 LIONS and TIGERS.

Amongst the recent additions to the Establishment, are the real Silken fantailed YAK, and the great BONASSUS, also the TASMANIAN DEVIL, and many other novelties, never before seen in this country.

The advert for Wombwell's menagerie from the *Darlington & Stockton Times* of early September 1866. It was during this visit that Frank was born.

Darlington Market Place, where the travelling menagerie had pitched its tents the day that Frank was born.

He was Frank Charles Bostock, and not only did he write the manual on how to tame a lion (published in 1903), but he was also the man who invented the circular big top. He was the man who trained a chimp to drive a car. He was the man who captured a lion that was prowling the sewers of Birmingham, terrorising Brummies with its roar. He was the man who introduced the boxing kangaroo to the world. He was the man who sent a crocodile over the Niagara Falls, he was the 'Animal King' who took America by storm in the 1890s.

He was born, according to the National Fairground Archive at Sheffield University, in the Market Place on 10 September 1866.

In the days before Sir David Attenborough started beaming all manner of exotic foreign animals onto our television screens, the only time ordinary people got to see them was when a menagerie rolled into town. The most famous travelling menagerie of the nineteenth century was started in Soho in 1804 by George Wombwell, who had acquired two boa constrictor snakes from London docks. In 1838, when his show was passing through Staffordshire, a twenty-four-year-old horseman called James Bostock was taken on to drive the wagons. James rose to become the show's contracting and advertising agent.

He may even have secured the booking that led to the menagerie arriving in Darlington Market Place on 11 November 1850.

'It is 18 years since the whole of this immense collection was exhibited in this town, since which time many large additions of highly interesting character have been made,' said the advert placed, perhaps by James, in the *Darlington & Stockton Times*.

Top of the bill was 'the Great Mandril – the wild man of South Africa'. This was probably a mandrill, a monkey with the sort of colouring on its bottom that would have to be viewed on a high definition TV set, or in real life, to appreciate fully.

Other attractions were 'elephants, hippopotamus, the Great Arctic Monsters, lions and lionesses, tiger and tigress, leopards, zebra or striped horse, striped or untameable hyenas, the Great Ursine Sloth of India, the Armadillo, and several Boa Constrictor serpents from Java'.

Wombwell's stayed in Darlington for several days, but by 16 November 1850, the show had reached Northallerton where seventy-three-year-old Mr Wombwell died, leaving the menagerie to his nieces. In 1852, James Bostock married one of those nieces, Emma Wombwell – he was thirty-eight and she was just eighteen.

On 8 September 1866, when the menagerie revisited Darlington, Emma was pregnant. 'Delimonico, the Arabian Lion Chief, will exhibit his Prussian Needle Gun, and drive the only pair of domesticated ZEBRAS in the world round the collection, prior to each performance with his 20 LIONS and TIGERS,' said the advert in the *D&S Times*.

A week later, the *D&S Times* reported: 'The performances by the elephant, the zebras, the leopards and the lions, directed by the famous Delimonico, were really wonderful. The Prussian needle-gun, presented to the lion tamer, was exhibited, and was the subject of general curiosity.'

Nowhere does it say what a Prussian needle-gun was, and nowhere does it mention that on the menagerie's second day in Darlington, Emma gave birth to a boy in her caravan in the Market Place.

Born on the road, baby Frank knew no other life than a peripatetic one. He took over the running of the menagerie, which he called Bostock and Wombwell's, and as his lion-taming skills grew, and his talent for self-publicity made his name well known, he had several shows touring the British provinces, the European mainland and the Australian outback, while he himself was tasting the big time in the United States.

He survived being savaged in 1901 in Indianapolis by his tiger, Rajah, and had another close shave in 1905 when Menelik the lion had a go at him. He died on 8 October 1912, aged forty-six, of flu when he was back in London.

'England's greatest showman dead', said the front-page headline in the *World's Fair* newspaper. 'The Animal King' is buried beneath a sleeping stone lion in Stoke Newington, and must be one of the most remarkable people to be born in Darlington.

Stephen 'Syd' Hall

In December 1937, George VI and his wife, Elizabeth, popped out from Windsor Castle to open a social club in nearby Slough. Elizabeth, still fondly remembered as 'the Queen Mother', spotted a new dartboard in the lounge, and said excitedly: 'Do let me try. I have heard so much about this game.'

In a quick three-dart match, she beat her husband by twenty-one points to nineteen.

What was good enough for the queen was good enough for women across the country, and suddenly the popularity of darts exploded.

This opened the door to Stephen Hall of Darlington, who was in his early thirties and worked at Cleveland Bridge. During the First World War, his father had been in the trenches where he had either been injured so his arm didn't work properly or he had been

The first and only World Pouff Dart Champion, Syd Hall, of Darlington.

The Arcade Cinema at the north end of Skinnergate was one of the venues where Syd thrilled audiences with his early displays of labial dexterity.

so restricted for space that he couldn't play darts properly. Either way, he had placed a dart sideways in his mouth and propelled it towards a dartboard. It was an update of an early nineteenth-century public house parlour game in which a 'puff-the-dart' man would blow a dart at a board of concentric circles through a blowpipe. The new version had the dart propelled by a combination of tongue power and spit force. Some people called it dart-spitting; the aficionados called it 'dart-pouffing'.

Stephen learned from his father, adopted the stage name 'Syd Hall' and turned the strange skill into a pub act, touring County Durham, earning beer money. He became associated with the cinemas on Skinnergate: the Court at the southern end (now shops) and the Arcade Cinema at the northern end (now a bingo hall). He would take to the front row of the circle and pouff his darts over the heads of the patrons below towards

The Arcade Cinema is today a bingo hall.

a dartboard which had been lowered in front of the screen. He would invariably hit the bullseye – from a distance of 36.5 feet.

But Syd was not a one-trick pony, a one-dart pouffer. He developed his act. A thread was stretched across the board on the cinema stage, and Syd pouffed his dart with such accuracy that it cut the thread in two. The audience could see his success, because the snapping of the thread caused a large message to unfurl across the screen: 'That's all, folks.'

The *Daily Mirror* in London heard of these curious goings-on in Darlington and, keen to pursue a new angle on the latest royal-endorsed fad, called upon the nation's 'pouffers', as it termed them, to take part in the first 'Pouff Darts Championship of Great Britain'.

Seven competitors arrived at the Dorchester Hotel on 18 March 1938 to compete for what was now being billed as a world title. Five of them were from the south-east, with Syd and Miss Edna Beattie – 'an attractive dark-haired young woman', according to the paper – coming from Darlington. Edna was the only female entrant.

The competitors stood 9 feet from the board – then the standard oche – and placed the darts sideways in their mouths. On the word 'blow', the contest commenced. According to the rules, they had 'ten goes of three pouffs each'.

Syd scored an impressive 644 points at an average of 17.89 and the *Mirror*, whose maths did not add up, anointed him the Pouff Darts Champion of the World. He won three guineas and a silver cup.

Inside the Arcade when it opened in August 1912.

An elated Syd said: 'All you need is a good pair of lungs. I have been playing on and off for about two years. It's a grand sport.'

The runner-up was Mr T. Baldwin, of Tunbridge Wells, and third place went to Edna, who, said the *Mirror*, had been 'swell in the picture' throughout the tournament.

'Her dark eyes dancing with fun', she told the paper: 'Gee, I'm so excited that I've got a prize. I have been playing for a month. I just retreated foot by foot until now I can blow a dart 20 feet.'

The paper's report of the inaugural world championship was headlined: 'P-o-u-f-f PLONK ... He is Darting to Fame', and Syd's name was made. He toured the cinemas and pubs of County Durham billed as the world champion and accompanied by a stooge called Curly Humble. He developed his act so that it included trick shots and 6-inch nails.

The *Mirror* did not hold a second Pouff Darts World Championship in 1939 – there were other, darker things on the nation's mind. The outbreak of the Second World War ended the fashion for darts and it became a pub game.

Syd died of lung cancer in 1956, but he passed his dart-pouffing secrets on to his nephew, Ron Tomlinson, who grew up in West Auckland. As the baton was handed from one generation to the next, the name of the skill changed. Pouffing was no more. Young Ron, aged just twelve at the start of the Second World War, was a dart blower, and he was discovered blowing a lit cigarette off his sister's head with a dart. They put him on the stage, and by the time he was thirteen, he was earning £2 a week in London's West End.

He performed under the name of Rondart, and he was billed as the 'world champion dart blower' or the 'modern William Tell'. In the 1950s, he appeared on stage with Stan Laurel, Frankie Vaughan, Frank Randle and Larry Grayson, and he blew darts so accurately that he could propel one into the neck of a bottle from 15 feet. Such skill took him around the world and put him on the telly. In 1965, he appeared on prime-time BBC1 on *Billy Smart's Circus*. In 1973, he blew a cigarette off Colin Crompton's head on the *Wheeltappers and Shunters Social Club*, and in 1985, he appeared on *The Paul Daniels Magic Show*.

His last TV appearance was on the Spanish version of the *Generation Game* in 1995. Having supported himself, and his Colombian wife, Cristina, through forty-plus years of professional dart-blowing, Rondart retired to Witton Park. He began writing his autobiography – tentatively entitled *I Blew It* – but it hadn't been published when he died, in his eighties, in 2005. He, of course, owed it all to Syd Hall, the first and only Pouff Dart Champion of the World, from Darlington.

DID YOU KNOW?
In 1939, Darlington had more cinema seats per head of population than any other town in Britain: Central Palace (1910–46, 710 seats), Empire (1911–60, 900), Arcade (1912–65, 800), Court (1913–47, 1,000), Scala (1913–62, 1,000), Gaumont (1913–62, 900), Majestic (1932–81, 1,600), Royal (1938, still going as the ABC, 700 seats) and Regent (1939–59, 1,050). Also showing films on some nights were the Mechanics Institute, the Larchfield Street Drill Hill, the New Hippodrome and the Northgate Astoria, plus the Lyric at Middleton St George (1936–59, 265 seats).